T0123251

THE UNIT
COMMANDER

Other Books by Sue Cullins Walls
The Cat Who Couldn't Purr
Who Killed Norma Jean?
The Mystery of the Cabin in the Woods
The Search
Reach the author at suewalls1475@aol.com

THE UNIT
COMMANDER

JIM RYAN'S STORY
BOOK 2 FSC SERIES - PART 1

SUE CULLINS WALLS

THE UNIT COMMANDER
JIM RYAN'S STORY

iUniverse books may be ordered through booksellers or by contacting:

iUniverse
1663 Liberty Drive
Bloomington, IN 47403
www.iuniverse.com
1-800-Authors (1-800-288-4677)

Because of the dynamic nature of the Internet, any web addresses or links contained in this book may have changed since publication and may no longer be valid. The views expressed in this work are solely those of the author and do not necessarily reflect the views of the publisher, and the publisher hereby disclaims any responsibility for them.

Any people depicted in stock imagery provided by Thinkstock are models, and such images are being used for illustrative purposes only. Certain stock imagery © Thinkstock.

ISBN: 978-1-5320-3400-8 (hc)
ISBN: 978-1-5320-3401-5 (e)

Print information available on the last page.

iUniverse rev. date: 10/25/2017

DEDICATION

This book is dedicated to all of the men and women who risk their lives every day to protect our country and keep it free from terrorists and others who would destroy our freedom. This includes all the military and Federal Agents, as well as all local and state police, Sheriffs Departments and, of course, the Homeland Security Agents.

ACKNOWLEDGMENTS

I wish to thank my husband, Harrison, again, for his patience while I wrote this book. As always, I also thank my sister, Joyce Price, for her encouragement and my brother, John Cullins, for the hard work of proofing my text. I especially want to thank my nephew, Dale Weatherman, Donna's husband, for his invaluable information. I also would like to thank my friends and family who have purchased my books and have said they enjoyed reading them.

DISCLAIMER

THE UNIT COMMANDER

The Federal Security Unit (FSU) is a fictional elite unit of the Federal Security Commission (FSC). The FSC is a fictional department of the Central Intelligence Agency (CIA).

Jim Ryan and Mark Fuller are fictional Unit Commanders of the fictional FSU. In this position, they are in charge of missions to combat foreign and domestic espionage, arrest perpetrators and protect citizens from all terrorist attacks, both foreign and domestic.

Due to the nature and secrecy of their missions, Jim Ryan would usually operate out of an office inside his home. He and Mark would report to their supervisor, who is located in the FSC Headquarters Building. They must give a report to their superior after the completion of each mission.

The FSC Board of Review is a fictional panel of authorities who are authorized to hear cases of charges against any of the officers who are employed by the FSC. Their decisions are final. They have the authority to either dismiss or reinstate a suspended officer.

There is no attempt by the author to depict any real department of the CIA. This book is a work of fiction. Names, characters, places and incidents (except for names of countries and military facilities mentioned) are the product of the author's imagination or are used fictitiously. Any resemblance to actual events, locales, or persons, living or dead, is coincidental.

My apologies to those who are reality purists in their works of fiction. I have taken the liberty to add some incidents that would probably not happen in real life. I have done this to add to the interest of the story. If I have gone a little too far out in left field for you, I apologize again, but, after all, it is fiction.

CHAPTER 1

A hero is an ordinary individual who finds the
strength to persevere and endure in spite of
overwhelming obstacles.-- Christopher Reeve

The honeymoon was over. Cat and Jim Ryan had spent two
wonderful weeks in Hawaii enjoying the peace and tranquility,
but Jim was anxious to get back home and get back to work. He was
the Unit Commander of an elite federal counter-espionage/counter-
terrorist unit (FSU), which is a unit within the Federal Security
Commission (FSC). He was a workaholic.

Cat, whose real name is Catherine, tried to get him to leave his
cell phone at the hotel when they were out sightseeing, but he said
he needed to stay in touch with his team, in case something came up
that they couldn't handle. He checked in with them every day and
everything was going well without him. That was probably what he
was afraid of, that they could get along without him.

When their plane landed, Mark Fuller and Ted Ames, two
of Jim's agents, were waiting to take Cat and Jim home. As soon
as they arrived at the cabin, Jim shut himself up in his office with
Mark and Ted. Jim had converted his home office into his command
headquarters earlier in his career, and since it was so convenient, he
just continued to use it as such.

Jim barely even unloaded their luggage before going back to
work. Cat was hurt that he would begin as soon as they arrived back

at home. Shortly, Jim, Mark and Ted came out of Jim's office. Jim kissed Cat and said "I have to go somewhere. I'll be back as soon as I can get back. I love you."

"Wait a minute," Cat said. "We just got home. You can't leave now."

"I'm sorry, Cat, but I have to go," he answered. "I'll be back as soon as possible."

Then he was gone. Cat sat down and cried. He had been gone a lot when he was looking for Olga Kinski, the Russian spy who had been trying to kill Cat, and also the hostage-takers, who had kidnapped her sisters, Carol and Charlotte, but they were in prison now. Cat wondered why he had to leave now, when they had just returned home from their honeymoon.

Cat had already decided to call Bill Hawkins, the newspaper editor of their local newspaper, and see if he had anything she could do. She had worked for him before the incident with Olga Kinski. She decided that this would be a good time to call him, since Jim was gone anyway.

Bill said that he had a part-time position open. He needed someone to gather small news items that could be used as fillers. They were usually human-interest stories that would be used. Cat said that she would love to do that, so he told her to be in his office on Monday morning and he would discuss hours and pay with her. Cat told him she would be there.

She wandered around the cabin, unpacking suitcases and putting things away. She also decided to wash their dirty laundry and fold it and put it away. The whole time she was doing this, she kept expecting Jim to come back home.

Since neither Barbara nor Molly, their two cooks, had come back to the cabin to work after Cat's and Jim's wedding, Cat fixed dinner and waited for Jim.

By 9:00 p.m., Jim hadn't returned, so Cat warmed up her dinner, ate and went upstairs to get ready for bed. At 10:00 p.m., she was exhausted, so she put on her nightgown and climbed into bed. She wondered if this was the way it would always be. She knew that he had worked late hours when he was trying to catch Olga Kinski, but she thought that after he had caught Olga, things would be different. About midnight, Jim came into the bedroom. He tried to undress quietly, but Cat wasn't asleep, so she turned on the bedside lamp.

"I'm sorry, Cat. Did I waken you?" he asked, surprised that she was still awake.

"No, I've been awake," she said. She was still angry that he had left and was gone so long. "Why couldn't you wait until Monday?" she asked angrily.

"Cat, I'm tired and I don't want to go into this now," he said. "You knew what kind of job I had when you married me. If you wanted someone with a 9:00 to 5:00 job, you should have married Matt." Matt was the man to whom she was engaged before she and Jim had become engaged.

When Cat gasped at that, he realized what he had said and grabbed her and held her to him and said, "I'm sorry, Cat. I didn't mean that. You married the right person. You should have married me. I'm the only one you should have married. I'm just tired. Can't this wait until morning? I just want to lie down and go to sleep."

Cat couldn't stay mad at him for long. She couldn't stand to see him in any kind of pain. "I'm sorry, Jim," she said. "I shouldn't have said anything. I know you must be tired. Good night. I love you."

"I love you, too, Cat, but sometimes you make me so angry," he said, as he crawled into bed. He kissed her and then he turned over on the other side of the bed and went sound asleep.

Cat turned off the lamp and turned over and faced the wall. She just prayed that every night wouldn't be like this one. Surely, it would get better. She loved him so much and she couldn't stand to be angry with him. "I just wanted him to hold me and kiss me like he did at one time," she thought. Soon she drifted off to sleep and the next thing she knew, it was morning.

When Cat went downstairs, she saw that Jim had brewed a pot of coffee and was sitting at the table drinking a cup.

"Good morning, Jim," she said, as she poured a cup of coffee for herself.

"Good morning, Hon," he answered. "Come here, I want to talk to you."

Cat poured creamer and sugar into her coffee and stirred it as she walked over to the table.

"I'm sorry about last night," Jim started. "I had to go. It was very important that I go. I'll try to make it up to you. I'll spend the whole day with you today. What would you like to do?"

"I just want to be with you," Cat said. "It doesn't really matter what we do."

After a few minutes, she said, "On second thought, why don't we go to the zoo? I haven't been there since I was a kid and I used to just love to go and watch all of the animals."

"Sure," he agreed. "That sounds like fun."

They walked arm-in-arm all around the zoo. Cat was having such a good time that she didn't notice a man taking a picture of them until Jim pushed her behind a tree and said, "Stay there until I come get you."

Before she could ask why, he was running after the man. Jim almost caught the man, but someone bumped into him and knocked him down. By the time Jim had gotten to his feet, the man had disappeared.

"What was that all about?" Cat asked when Jim returned to retrieve her.

"I don't like anyone taking my picture when I'm with you," he answered. "He had to be up to something. I just hope I haven't put you in danger."

"What kind of danger?" Cat asked. She was a little frightened now since Jim seemed so concerned.

"Don't worry, Hon," he said. "It was probably nothing. He probably just wanted a picture of a beautiful girl. I'm sure that's all it was."

As Jim said that, he turned and looked behind them. He had

a worried look on his face, so his words didn't give Cat much confidence.

"Come on, Hon," he said as he took her arm and headed toward the exit. "Let's go home now. I'm still pretty tired. I'll have to go back to work Monday and I need to rest."

When they got back home, Jim seemed a little paranoid about the man taking their picture. He said Cat couldn't go outside by herself anymore. If she wanted to go somewhere, she had to wait until he was able to take her. She felt like she had gone back in time to the time before Olga Kinski had been put into prison.

Cat asked him if Olga or some of her gang had escaped from prison. He assured her that they were all still in prison. He told her not to worry, but she still couldn't go anywhere without him, Mark or one of the other members of his team with her. Cat felt like a prisoner all over again.

"Jim," she said that night. "I can't go through this again. If something happens to me, it'll just have to happen. I can't just sit here and wait for you all day long. I have an appointment with Bill Hawkins next week. He thinks he may have something for me to do."

"No, Cat," Jim said. "You're not going to go to work. Not yet anyway. Not until I find out why that guy was photographing us."

The next day was Sunday. Cat and Jim attended Landmark Baptist Church, the local Baptist church where they had gone all of their lives. They hadn't gone to church while they were having the problem with Olga Kinski and her gang, so it really felt good to be in church again. That started the week off on a good note.

On Monday morning, after breakfast, Cat got ready to go see Mr. Hawkins.

"Where do you think you're going?" Jim asked.

"I told Bill Hawkins, the editor of the paper, that I would come see him today," she answered. "He said he might have a part-time job for me."

"I told you you're not going anywhere without me, Mark or one of my men with you," Jim said. "Not until I find out what that guy was doing. You might as well get used to it."

"Well, you can just come with me, then, because I'm going," Cat said, as her stubbornness returned.

"No, Cat," he said, as he grabbed her arm. "I mean it. You're not going anywhere until I make sure it's safe for you to leave here."

Cat didn't say anything else, but she gave him a look that could melt an iceberg.

He pulled her to his chest and kissed the top of her head. "I love you, Cat, more than anything else in this world. If anything ever happened to you, I couldn't go on living. Why can't you just do as I say for once in your life? I know what I'm talking about. That guy was up to no good. I have to keep you safe."

Now Cat really felt bad for the way she was acting. "I'm sorry, Jim," she said humbly. "I'll just call Bill and tell him I can't come in today."

"Tell him you don't know when you'll be able to come in, while you're at it," Jim said.

Cat gave him a mean look, but said, "OK" and picked up the phone to make the call. She told Bill that she wasn't able to take the job right now, but she would get back in touch with him when she could. He said that it was OK, that he would find someone else. He said that he was sorry that she was unable to take the job. "I was looking forward to working with you again, but I understand that sometimes we can't do what we would like to do."

Jim went into his office to work, so Cat went upstairs to their bedroom. Since Barbara, the cook, and Mildred, the housekeeper, had now returned and did everything, there was nothing for Cat to do. She had a computer in their bedroom, so she decided to log onto Facebook and see what Carol and Charlotte, her two sisters, were doing.

Carol and Skip had decided to stay in Hawaii another week for their honeymoon. They knew that when they returned to college, they would be very busy, so they wanted to get as much rest as they could.

Charlotte and Tyler were already working on their new movie. She told Cat that the filming was going great. Cat could hardly wait for them to finish filming it, so she could see it. She had seen their first movie, "The Princess of the Forest," and it was very good.

Shortly, Jim knocked on the bedroom door and came into the room. "Cat, I need to leave for a while," he said. "One of my men will be here soon. He'll stay with you while I'm gone. You do as he says, now. Don't give him any trouble."

Cat started to say something, but he gave her a kiss and hurried out the door. She heard him run down the stairs and out the door and then he was gone.

"Jim Ryan," she said under her breath. "You are the most aggravating one man I have ever met."

After a couple of hours passed and there was no sign of any of Jim's team, Cat assumed that he had changed his mind and decided not to send anyone. That made her feel pretty good.

"I guess he decided to trust me, after all," Cat said to herself.

Then there was a loud knock on the door. When she answered it, there was a man she didn't know standing there.

"Ms. Cat, I'm Dan, one of Jim's men," he said.

"Come on in," Cat said as she stepped back to let him in.

"I've come to get you," he said. "Jim's been hurt. I'm supposed to take you to the hospital."

"Let me grab my purse," Cat said, as she ran up the stairs. Her heart was racing. She came back down by way of the kitchen and told Barbara that Jim was in the hospital and she was going to see about him.

Cat didn't even hesitate before getting into the car with the stranger. As much as Jim had cautioned her, she should have, but she didn't.

When Dan pulled up in front of a building, Cat said, "This isn't the hospital. Where are you taking me?"

"It's OK, Girlie," he said, with a smirk, as he stuck a gun in her face. "You'll find out soon enough. Now, get out of the car and do as I say."

Cat looked for a place to run, but Dan grabbed her arm and pulled her up the steps and into the building. She struggled to get away, but he pushed her inside. Then she heard Jim shout, "Cat." When she looked over, she saw Jim, tied to a chair. His face was bruised and bleeding.

"Jim," she cried and tried to run over to him, but Dan held her back and wouldn't let her go.

"Not now, Girlie," he said and smirked again.

Then Cat saw Mark lying on the floor with blood oozing from a wound in his head. He looked like he was unconscious.

"Let her go," Jim threatened. "If you hurt her, I'll kill you, if it's the last thing I do."

"You talk tough, Mr. Federal Agent, but you're in no position to kill anyone," Dan said, as he put his arm around Cat's waist.

"Now, if you don't tell us what we want, your pretty little wife may not be so pretty after I get through with her," Dan said, as he gave Cat an evil grin.

Jim tried to stand up, but the man behind him hit him on the head with the butt of a gun.

"No," Cat screamed. "Leave him alone. Let me go."

Cat struggled with Dan, but it was no use. He was a lot stronger than she was and he had a really tight hold on her waist.

"Please let me go to Jim," Cat pleaded.

"Look, Girlie," Dan said, with a sneer. "I didn't bring you here so you could cuddle up to Mr. Federal Agent. I brought you here to get him to talk. Now, everything will be a lot better for you and your hero, if you just convince him to tell us what we want to know."

Then, as he waved the gun at Jim, he said, "Now, Mr. Federal Agent. do you want to cooperate or do we hurt your beautiful wife. I think I could have some fun with her while you decide." He then started trying to kiss Cat and she tried to turn her head to avoid him.

"Leave her alone," Jim shouted again and struggled to get the ropes untied.

"You just give me what I want and I may give you back your pretty wife," Dan said, as he held Cat tighter and gave an ugly laugh.

Cat heard Mark moan and thanked God that he wasn't dead. She had been afraid that they had killed him. His head was still bleeding and he put a hand to it and said, "Ouch."

"Don't move," Dan said as he waved the gun in Mark's direction.

"Ben, get over there and tie that one up. He may be hurt, but he could still cause us some problems," Dan said.

Ben hurried over and jerked Mark's hands behind him and tied him tight.

Cat started praying for God to help them out of this bad situation. She couldn't see how they were going to get out of it otherwise. She knew God could do something.

He had always helped her get out of bad situations in the past so she trusted Him to do so now.

Now Dan turned his attention back to Jim.

"OK, Mr. Federal Agent," he said. "This is your last chance. Give us the code or you're never going to see your pretty wife again. Like I said, I think I'll just have a little fun with her while you decide."

With that, he turned Cat around and started to kiss her again. She turned her face to the side and tried to get away from him, but he was again too fast for her.

He slapped her hard on the cheek and said, "No, no, Girlie. You can't leave now. The fun has just begun."

Jim jumped up with the chair tied to him and lunged for Dan. Dan hit him on the head again and Cat pulled free and ran for the door. Jim rolled over under Dan's feet and tripped him when he tried to run after Cat. Ben saw what was happening and started after Cat, but she made it to the door before he could catch her.

She had no idea where she was, but she just started running. She didn't know what had happened to Jim, but she hoped that he was all right. At least if she could get away, they couldn't use her to make him do something he didn't want to do.

Cat hid in a large culvert on the side of the road and heard Ben running around looking for her. Her face ached where Dan had hit her and a trickle of blood ran down her cheek. She wiped the blood away with the back of her hand. She figured she would probably have a black eye in the morning. She didn't know how long she hid there, but it was beginning to get dark when she cautiously crept out. She had her cell phone in her pocket so she called 911. She tried to explain to the dispatcher that she had been kidnapped and had escaped her captors. The dispatcher said that she needed an address and Cat told her she didn't know where she was. Since it was becoming dark, Cat could just barely make out some landmarks around her. She gave the dispatcher what she could see and the dispatcher said that by tracing Cat's cell phone and the landmarks she had given her, she could figure out where Cat was.

While Cat was waiting for the police, someone came up behind her, grabbed her and put a hand over her mouth.

"Cat, it's me, Jim," he whispered in her ear.

"Thank God you're all right," Cat said and tried to turn to face him.

"Don't, you don't want to see me right now. Come on we're getting out of here," he said as he pulled Cat along with him. He was going so fast, she stumbled and almost fell. He caught her and, when he did, she noticed the blood on his hand.

"We need to get out of here as fast as we can," he said, as he kept dragging Cat along. "Mark's waiting in the car. Come on."

They got to the car and Jim pushed Cat into the back seat and then he jumped into the front seat with Mark. As soon as he shut the door, Mark gunned the engine and took off at a high rate of speed.

When they finally got home, Jim helped Cat out of the car and into the cabin. When he turned on the lights, Cat gasped. His face was a bloody mess. She could hardly even recognize him. Both of his hands were cut and bleeding and his face was bruised and bleeding.

"Cat, you're bleeding," he said as he gently touched her injured cheek.

"I'm OK. Let me help you," Cat said, as she touched his swollen face.

"No," he said as he jerked away at her touch. "I have to do it myself. Go on up to bed. I'll be up as soon as I clean up a little." Then he walked toward the downstairs bathroom. Cat gave up and went on upstairs to their bedroom.

She looked at herself in the bathroom mirror. She was a mess, too. Her hair was a tangled mess and she had dirt all over her. Her face was scratched and there were drops of dried blood in spots. "Yes, I'm pretty sure I'll have a black eye in the morning," she thought.

Cat started running hot water into the tub and started undressing. As she lay soaking in the hot water, she heard Jim come into the bedroom. He stuck his head in at the door and asked if she was all right.

"I am now that we're home," she said. "I'm going to soak for a long time before going to bed."

"Cat, I'm sorry that you had to go through that," Jim said, as he came and knelt down beside the tub.

Cat looked at him and gasped again. He looked even worse now than he had looked before. His handsome face was all cut and bleeding and he had two black eyes and a swollen lip.

"Oh, Jim," she said. "You look terrible."

"I feel terrible," he said. "Now you know why I've been so insistent that you always have someone with you when you go out, don't you? I should never have married you," he said dejectedly. "I knew that some day this would happen. I just didn't think it would be this soon."

"Don't say that, Jim," Cat said. "I don't care what happens to me, as long as I'm with you. I love you. I've always loved you. You have made me the happiest woman alive just to be your wife."

"Cat, I love you more than anything in the world and I can't stand that I put you in that kind of danger," he said, as he leaned over and kissed her and caressed her sore face.

"It'll all work out," she said. "Now go on and let me get dry and I'll meet you in the bedroom."

When Cat walked into the bedroom, Jim was lying on top of the covers looking up at the ceiling. "Cat," he said, when he saw her. "If it's the last thing I do, I'll get him for putting his filthy hands on you and hurting you. I mean it, Cat. I'll get him."

"I know you will, Jim," Cat said. "But right now you're going to let me doctor those cuts." She got some medicine and cotton balls and daubed a little on each cut. Each time she daubed, Jim winced.

"I'm sorry if I'm hurting you," Cat said, "but you need some medicine on them so they won't get infected."

He took her hand and kissed it. "I know, Cat, and I thank you. Since Mother died, I haven't had anyone who cared enough to doctor my wounds. Thanks."

Cat almost cried when he said that. She had forgotten that he had lost his parents when he was still in high school. Cat thought, "I should have been caring for him all those years, but I never even thought about it."

When she was finished putting medicine on his cuts, he pulled her down and kissed her. "Now let me doctor your wound," he told her.

"Have I told you how much I love you?" he said, as he gently daubed medicine on her face. Then he kissed her and kept kissing her until she was lost in his love. Afterwards, he rolled over and went to sleep. Cat got up and spread a blanket over him and went to sleep beside him. It had been a long, tiring day.

CHAPTER 2

The next morning after breakfast, Jim went into his office and shut the door. Soon, he opened the door and called Cat into his office.

"Can you type?" he asked.

"Yes, I can," she replied.

He showed Cat his hands. They were still swollen from all the cuts and bruises. "I can't use my hands," he said. "Will you type my report for me?"

"Sure," she said. "Just tell me how to do it and what to say."

They spent all morning in his office. He dictated and Cat typed. Cat was on cloud nine, since he had finally let her help him do something.

After that, he had Cat do all of his typing until his hands were well. She learned a lot about some of the things he had been doing when he would leave and be gone for so long.

When he finally got over being so sore and his hands had healed, he took her to the rifle range and taught her how to shoot a pistol and a rifle. He said he didn't want her to ever be at the mercy of someone like Dan again. He also bought her a small pistol to carry in her purse.

"I want you to keep this with you at all times, now that you know how to use it. I want you to use it when you need to," he said. Jim then took Cat to a self-defense class and stayed and watched to make sure she learned how to defend herself properly.

One day after Cat had learned to shoot as well as he thought that she should and was able to protect herself, he suggested that she try to get a job with the FSC. He said that he would be her Commander and he would be with her on every assignment. Cat thought that would be wonderful. Then she would be able to be with him when he went away and wouldn't have to sit at home and worry about him.

There were times when he said that she couldn't go with him on an assignment, though. One of those times came one warm September day. The leaves had already begun to change colors and the weather was almost perfect. Jim came out of his office, after being closed up with Mark and Ted for about an hour.

"Hon, I have to go away for a while," he said, as he kissed Cat goodbye. "I don't know when I'll return. Mark is going with me, but I'll leave Ted here to protect you. Now, you do as Ted says, OK?"

"But, Jim," Cat whined. "Why can't I go with you? You said that I was really good at shooting and I can protect myself really well now."

"Not this time, Hon," he said. "This is something that you can't do."

Then he and Mark left.

"I have a location on Dan Orretese, the one who captured us last month," Jim said, as he and Mark drove out of the yard. "The team has already gotten him holed up in Winchester. That's about a two-hour drive from here. When we get there, I want to have him to myself for a while."

"Jim, don't do anything foolish," Mark advised him. "I know what he did to you and Cat, but you have to remember your position. I would like to do something to him, too, for this cut on my head, but I know that's not possible."

"Mark," Jim said through clenched teeth. "You just let me have him alone for a while. You don't even have to watch. That way you won't be involved."

"Jim, don't do it, please," Mark pleaded, but he didn't even faze him. Jim was determined to do what he had set out to do.

When Jim and Mark got to the building where his team had Dan Orretese and his gang cornered, Jim and Mark took their positions.

"Come on, men" Jim said as he cautiously ran toward the building.

There was a gun battle and finally Jim was able to get inside the building.

"Federal agents," Jim called as he, Mark and the others stormed the building.

"Throw your guns down and put your hands in the air," Jim demanded.

Mark and the others then put handcuffs on everyone except Orretese.

"Leave him," Jim commanded. "Take all the others to the cars."

"Jim, don't," Mark made one last plea.

"You gonna shoot an unarmed man?" Orretese asked.

"No, I'm going to put my gun over here," Jim said, as he lay his gun down.

"Mark, you watch him," Jim said. Then he told Orretese to try to escape. "Go for the gun. Try to escape," Jim told Orretese again.

"No," Orretese said. "You'll shoot me."

"I can't shoot you. I don't have a gun. See," Jim said, as he opened his jacket and showed Orretese that he had no other weapon.

When Orretese refused to try to run, Jim shouted at him, "Hit me, then."

"No," Orretese said.

"I said hit me," Jim said even louder. "What's wrong? You didn't have any problem hitting me when I was tied to a chair. You even hit me with a gun. Is that the problem? You need a gun to hit me with? Give him a gun, Mark."

"No, Jim," Mark said. "Don't do this."

"I said give him a gun, Mark," Jim said through clenched teeth. "That's an order."

"No, Jim," Mark said again. "Think about what you're doing. You're not thinking straight."

"I'll get it myself," Jim said, as he walked over and picked up his own revolver and threw it down at Orretese's feet. "Pick it up." Jim said.

"No," Orretese said.

"I said pick it up," Jim shouted again. "If you don't pick it up, you're dead anyway," Jim said.

Then Orretese reached over and picked up the gun.

"Now hit me," Jim said again.

This time Orretese hit Jim. Orretese figured that Jim was going to kill him, anyway, so he tried to shoot him.

Jim kicked the gun out of Orretese's hand and hit him hard on the jaw. Then Jim let Orretese hit him again.

"You put your filthy hands on my wife," Jim said as he hit Orretese again, even harder than he did before. "Don't you ever even look at my wife again. If I catch you even looking at her, you're a dead man," Jim said between hits.

"I'm reporting you," Orretese said through bloody lips.

"I don't care what you do, but if you ever, I mean ever, touch my wife again, you're a dead man." With each word that Jim said, he hit Orretese again a little harder.

"Jim, stop," Mark said. "You don't know what you're doing. You can get into a lot of trouble. You're not thinking straight."

When Jim finally knocked Orretese unconscious, he grabbed him by the collar and dragged him to his feet.

"Now," Jim said, as he shook him back to consciousness. "Do you want to file a complaint?"

Orretese looked at the hate in Jim's eyes and knew that Jim could very well kill him right there. "No, no, I don't," he said.

"Come on, Mark," Jim said, as he dragged Orretese to his car. "I'm taking him in myself."

When they got to the station, Jim took Orretese to the booking room while the others took the rest of the suspects in.

"This is the man who kidnapped Mark and me," Jim said to the officer in charge. "I want to charge him with kidnapping, assault and espionage."

"He looks like he's in pretty bad shape, Jim," the officer said, when he saw all of the cuts, bruises and blood on Orretese's face. "Did you have trouble arresting him?"

"He resisted arrest," Jim said flatly.

"He resisted, did he?" the officer asked.

"Yes, he resisted," was all the explanation Jim gave.

Jim gave Orretese a shove and started to walk away. "Come on, Mark," Jim said as he headed toward the exit

"Mark, wait a minute," the officer said.

When Mark walked back to see what the officer wanted, he asked, "What about that, Mark? I know he was the one who held you and Jim captive for a while, but did he resist bad enough to look like this?"

"Like Jim said," Mark answered. "He resisted arrest. Jim had to subdue him the only way he could. He could have shot him, you know." Then he followed Jim out the door.

When they were in the car headed toward home, Mark said, "Jim, I know how you feel about Cat. I feel the same way, but you're treading on dangerous ground. Not only can you be fired, you could go to prison yourself."

"He's just lucky I didn't kill him," Jim said angrily. "If anyone else touches or hits her like he did, they're dead."

The rest of the trip was made in silence. Mark had warned Jim and he felt like he had done his duty toward him. He just hoped that nothing became of it. He would hate to see Jim's brilliant career end in shame. He was a great guy with which to work. He was hard as nails, but he always had your back. Mark just hoped that he hadn't revealed too much about how he felt about Cat to Jim. He had accidentally let that slip.

When they walked into the cabin, Cat immediately saw the cuts and blood on Jim's face. "Jim, you're hurt," she cried, as she ran to him. "Let me put something on those cuts."

"It's OK. You should see the other guy," he replied, as he gave a wry laugh.

"Mark, you and Ted can go now, if you wish," Jim said, looking at Mark. "You can either go on home or come back here for the night after you have some fun."

"I think I'll come back here, since I have to be here for my report in the morning, anyway," Mark said. "Come on, Ted, let's go have some fun. You want to come, too, Jim?"

"No, I'll just stay here and have fun with Cat," he said with a grin and a wink at Cat.

"How did it go?" Ted asked Mark, as they were walking out the door.

"I'll tell you in the car," Mark answered.

After they were in the car and Mark started the engine, Ted asked again, "What happened?"

"Everything went just as we planned it until we got inside and Jim saw the guy who was holding Cat," Mark began. "Then Jim lost it. He laid his gun down and started beating up the guy. He kept wanting the guy to fight back, but he just let Jim pummel him. If he hadn't passed out when he did, I think Jim would have killed him."

"Gee, I never thought Jim would have done something like that," Ted said.

"Well, you know how he feels about Cat," Mark answered. "Maybe he's too attached to her, if he goes off the deep end like that just because a guy touches her. Well, he did more than touch her, but you know what I mean."

"Yeah, well you better not ever even think about touching her," Ted said.

"Don't worry," Mark answered. "As much as I would love to hold her and kiss her, I wouldn't even be alone with her, if I didn't have to at times."

"What do you mean you would love to hold her and kiss her, Mark?" Ted asked.

"I mean just that," Mark said.

"You better be careful, Mark," Ted said. "You got feelings for the wrong woman. Don't let Jim find out how you feel about Cat."

"I know that, Ted," Mark said. "Sometimes you can't help who you fall in love with, though. Do you understand that?"

"Yeah, I understand. Just be careful and don't let Jim find it out," Ted said.

"Well, enough about that, let's go and have some fun," Mark said. He decided that he had better be more careful from now on. He hoped that he hadn't made a mistake in letting Ted know how he felt about Cat. He could hold that against him some day.

Back at the cabin, Jim said he was going upstairs to take a shower. Cat followed him up the stairs. "When you get through, I'll doctor your cuts, OK?" she asked, not knowing whether he would let her or not. When he came out of the shower, she made him sit on the edge of the bed while she daubed medicine on his cuts.

"Ouch, Cat," he said as he drew away from her hand. "Don't be so rough."

"For someone as tough and macho as you are, you sure do flinch at a little antiseptic," she said.

"That's enough antiseptic for now. Come here," he said, as he pulled her to him and lay back on the bed. Then he rolled over and kissed her.

"I love you, Cat," he said and kissed her again. "You know I would do anything for you don't you?"

"I love you, too, Jim," she answered, and I would do anything for you."

That was the last thing she said before he silenced her with more kisses and they became one. Then he rolled over and went to sleep.

She slipped out of bed and into the shower. After her shower, she dressed and gently shook Jim.

"Honey," she said. "I think Barbara has dinner ready. Are you hungry?"

"I'm hungry for you," he said as he grabbed her and kissed her again. "I guess I am a little hungry. I haven't eaten since breakfast. Let's go see what Barbara has fixed."

That night, Cat was awake when she heard Mark and Ted come up the stairs to their rooms. They were laughing and talking. They sounded as if they had had a good time. Jim had been asleep, but he awoke at the sound of their voices.

"Can you believe that Cassidy Love?" Cat heard Mark ask Ted, as they headed toward their rooms. "She's some hot chick, isn't she?" She didn't hear what Ted's answer was, because they had reached their rooms and had closed the doors behind them.

"They just now getting in?" Jim asked. "What time is it?"

"It looks like it's about 3:00 a.m.," Cat answered.

"I guess they must have had a really good time," Jim said. "I hope they're able to work in the morning."

Then he put an arm around Cat and pulled her to him. He kissed her and said, "Did I ever tell you how much I love you?"

"Yes, but you can tell me again," Cat replied.

"I love you, Cat," he said dreamily. "More than you'll ever know."

Then he turned over and went back to sleep.

The next morning, Mark and Ted were late coming down to breakfast, so Jim finished his breakfast and headed for his office.

"Tell the guys to come to my office when they finish breakfast, will you, Cat?" he asked. "I need to get our reports finished and sent off."

After Mark and Ted finished breakfast, they went into Jim's office.

"How do you want to handle this?" Mark asked Jim.

"Tell it the way you saw it," Jim answered. "I don't want you to lie for me. He attacked my wife and I had to arrest him. When he resisted arrest, I had no other choice but to subdue him. That's what

I said, but you say what you observed. I don't expect you to lie for me. If you think I handled anything incorrectly, then I want you to report it. That's the way I trained you. I intend for you to be honest in your report. Don't let our friendship cloud your judgment. If you think I did something wrong, I expect you to say so."

When he finished his report, Mark handed it to Jim to read. After reading it, Jim looked at Mark and asked, "Is this how you saw it? When the suspect would not submit to being handcuffed, Commander Ryan had no other alternative but to subdue him," Jim read out loud. "You will swear under oath that that is the way you saw it?"

"Yes, Jim," Mark said again. "That's how I saw it."

Jim was silent for a few minutes and then he sighed and attached his report to Mark's and slipped them into an envelope.

"I think I'll take these to headquarters personally," Jim said. "I may have to answer some questions. I might as well get it over with."

When Jim and Mark got to headquarters, Agent Nash said that Director Halbert wanted to see them.

"Come in Jim, Mark," Director Halbert said when Jim knocked on his office door. "Sit down. Do you have your report from yesterday?"

"Yes, Sir, I brought it in person," Jim answered.

"Let me have it," Director Halbert said, as he took the papers and started reading them immediately. After he finished reading, he looked at Jim and was silent for a few minutes, while he mulled over what he had read.

"Jim, one of the suspects made a complaint against you," Director Halbert said. "Do you know anything about a complaint?"

"No, Sir," was all Jim said.

"Can you explain to me why one of the suspects was bruised and bleeding, but none of the others were?" the director asked.

Jim took a deep breath and paused for a few minutes before answering. "He attacked my wife, Director Halbert," Jim finally said.

"He attacked your wife?" Director Halbert asked. "How and when did he attack your wife?"

"He kidnapped her and brought her to where he was holding Mark and me. He tried to make me talk by abusing her. He hit her. He gave her a black eye," Jim answered.

"Is she here?" the director wanted to know.

"No, she isn't, Sir," Jim answered.

"I need to talk to her," Director Halbert said. "Can you get her in sometime this afternoon?"

"Do you have to talk to her, Sir?" Jim asked. "I really don't want to put her through anything else like that."

"Yes, I need to talk to her," he answered. "If I don't have her to back up your story, then I'll have to make my decision based on Mark's and your report and what Mr. Orretese said. I'm telling you, Jim, it doesn't look good for you."

"Will my record be taken into consideration?" Jim asked.

When Director Halbert said, "Yes, of course it will," Jim said, "Then I'm sorry, but I can't put my wife through that again."

"You know you'll probably be suspended and you could be given a prison sentence, don't you?" Director Halbert said.

"I understand, Sir," Jim answered.

"OK, Jim, I'll delay my decision until you have had time to consider the consequences of what you're doing," the director said. "Maybe by this afternoon you may change your mind about bringing your wife in. Let me know if you change your mind. I'll give you until Monday morning." Then he rose and walked to the door and opened it. "I'll expect to hear from you soon. Good day."

Jim and Mark walked out of the Director's office and they both gave a sigh at the same time.

"Well, that went well," Jim said sarcastically.

"Jim, you're crazy," Mark said, as they walked to the exit. "He was giving you an out. Why didn't you take it?"

"I can't put Cat through that," Jim answered. "She is already traumatized enough. I don't want to traumatize her even more."

"If she knew that it meant you might get a prison sentence, she would gladly do it for you," Mark said. "I know her well enough to know she would."

"Yes, I know she would, too, but I'm not going to put her through it," Jim said adamantly.

"Jim, I think you're making a mistake," Mark argued.

"If my record doesn't mean anything, then I've wasted my whole life with the FSC," Jim said, as they got into the car. "I'm not putting the woman I love through that, if my record doesn't mean a thing. Now, you drive us home and don't say another word about it, OK?"

Mark did as Jim said and drove straight back to the cabin, but he still felt that Jim needed to do something to defend himself. Jim had been a good boss all the years he had been working for him and he didn't want to see him go out in shame.

When they got back to the cabin, Jim went into his office and shut the door without asking Mark to come into it with him. Mark felt that this would be a good chance to talk to Cat.

"Hi, Mark," Cat said, as she came out of the den. "Didn't Jim come back with you?"

"Yeah, he went into his office," Mark answered. "Wait a minute," he said, when he saw her headed toward Jim's office. "I need to talk to you a minute," Mark continued.

"Cat, Jim would beat me up if he knew I told you, but I can't let him do what he's doing."

"What do you mean, Mark?" Cat asked.

"Come here into the kitchen. I don't want him to know I said anything to you," Mark said, as he steered her toward the kitchen.

"Jim did something that is frowned upon in our line of work," Mark began.

"What?" Cat started, but Mark put a finger to her lips and said, "Just listen. Don't say anything. That guy that was holding you that day we were kidnapped," Mark continued. "You know the one I mean?"

"Yes," Cat said and involuntarily shuddered.

"Yeah, you know who I mean. I can tell by the way you look. Anyway, we captured him yesterday," Mark continued.

"You did!" Cat exclaimed.

"Quiet, he'll hear you," Mark said, putting a finger on her lips again.

"Jim really roughed him up. More than he should have." Mark lowered his voice then to make sure only Cat could hear him.

"Cat, where are you?" Jim called, coming out of his office.

"Wait, maybe he won't come in here," Mark said, holding her back.

"Cat, where are you?" Jim called again.

"I'm in here, Jim," she said, as she pulled her arm out of Mark's grasp and headed toward Jim.

"What are you doing in the kitchen?" Jim asked. Then he saw Mark. "Mark," he said angrily. "What were you doing with my wife?"

"We were just having a friendly chat," Mark answered and started to walk by Jim. Jim caught his arm and gave him an angry look. Mark shrugged and walked on into the den.

"What did he say to you, Cat?" Jim wanted to know.

"Nothing, Jim," Cat said. "He just started to tell me something, but you interrupted. What is it all about?"

"It's nothing that you need to worry your pretty little head about," Jim said, as he kissed her. "Just forget it. Mark was sticking his nose in where it doesn't belong."

Then he walked into the den where Mark was waiting. "Mark, will you come into my office with me for a few minutes?" he said.

"Look, Jim, I was just..." Mark started, as the door closed on them.

"I know what you were just trying to do," Jim said through clenched teeth. "I told you to leave it alone. Now, Cat will want to know what you were talking about. She'll pester me to death and eventually I'll have to tell her something. I wish you hadn't done that."

"Jim, you can't just quit and let Orretese win," Mark insisted. "That wouldn't be doing justice to Cat or us either. Can't you see? You have to do something or he'll win. It'll be just like he's abusing her again."

Jim didn't say anything for several minutes. "I sure made a mess of things didn't I? I guess I should have handled it differently. I just couldn't stand the fact that he did that to Cat and I couldn't punish him myself. Can't you see, Mark? I had to do it myself. If I didn't, I couldn't stand to look her in the face anymore."

"Tell her what you did, Jim," Mark said. "I'm sure she'll understand. You're not giving her enough credit. I think she'll go with you to the Director's office. She deserves to be given a chance. After all, she loves you very much and I know she wouldn't want to see you disgraced like you're going to be if you continue like you're going."

"All right, you win," Jim finally agreed. "I'll think about it."

"Don't just think about it," Mark said. "Do it."

Then Jim opened the door and called, "Cat, Hon, can you come here for a minute?"

"Yes, Jim," she said, as she hurried toward Jim's office.

"Cat, Hon, sit down." Jim motioned to a chair and Cat sat down.

"I don't know how to begin," he said hesitantly. "I really did a stupid thing." Then he paused.

"What did you do, Jim?" Cat asked.

"I brought my personal feelings into the apprehension of a suspect."

"What does that mean?" Cat asked.

"I beat up that guy, that Dan Orretese guy," Jim said finally. "You know the one who, you know the one who? I can't say it." Jim was having a hard time saying it.

"I know who you mean, Jim," Cat said, as she stood up and walked over to Jim and put a hand on his shoulder. "I understand."

"No, you don't understand, Cat," Jim said, as he ran his fingers through his hair.

"I beat up an unarmed prisoner. That's grounds for dismissal and maybe a prison sentence depending on how lenient the court is with me."

"Oh, Jim, no," Cat cried. "Why?"

"Because he put his filthy hands on you. He hurt you," Jim cried in anguish.

"Oh, Jim," Cat said and she put her arms around Jim and cried on his shoulder.

After a few minutes, Jim pushed her away and held her at arms length. "I had to do it, Cat," he said. "I couldn't live with myself if I didn't. I couldn't look you in the eye again, knowing I had a chance to punish him and didn't."

"What happens, now?" Cat asked.

"I don't know. Director Halbert wants to talk to you. I told him I didn't want to put you through that. I can't let him put you through it," Jim said.

"Will it make any difference to the outcome, if I talk to him?" Cat asked.

"I don't know," Jim answered. "You may go through the trauma of reliving it and then I'll still be dismissed or it may help. I just don't know. That's why I didn't want you to get involved. I wouldn't have told you about it, if Mark hadn't stuck his nose into my business."

"I couldn't let you just throw years of work away like that, Jim," Mark said. "You're a great Commander and I hate to see you just go down in disgrace."

"Well, I still might, even if Cat does talk to the Director," Jim said. "Then I wouldn't have accomplished anything."

"I want to talk to the Director, Jim," Cat said. "Maybe it'll help. I know for sure that if I don't talk to him, we will have missed a chance for me to help."

"OK, enough of this," Jim said, perking up. "We can't do anything now, because the Director is probably gone by now. We'll go in the morning. Come on, let's see what Barbara has for us to eat."

So they all went back to the kitchen to see if Barbara had

anything prepared. She, of course, had prepared a meal fit for a king. They sat down at the table in the dining room and Jim said grace. Then they ate.

That night when they went to bed, Cat asked, "What happened, Jim. Tell me about it."

"There's not a lot to tell, Cat," Jim said flatly. "I beat up the guy until I knocked him unconscious. I told him if he ever touched you again, I'd kill him. I told him, if he even looked at you again, I'd kill him. What more do you want to know?"

"I guess that's enough," Cat said. "I'm sorry I asked. Did you realize the consequences when you did that?"

"Yes, I did," Jim answered. "I knew exactly what would happen to me, but I think he'll think twice before he puts a hand on you or hits you again. Now, forget it and go to sleep. There's nothing you can do about it tonight." Then he kissed her and turned his back to her and went to sleep.

Cat turned over, too, and said a prayer. "Please, God. Help things work out for Jim. He really loves his job. I don't know what he would do if he got dismissed. I sure don't know what I'd do if he went to prison, especially since it would be because of me."

Then she lay there looking at the wall all night, dreading what would happen in the morning. Then she told herself that she just had to have faith that God would make everything right.

CHAPTER 3

The next morning after breakfast, Jim, Cat and Mark went to see the Director of the Federal Security Commission (FSC). When they arrived, Director Halbert said he wanted to talk to Cat alone at first.

After they were settled, the Director said, "Now, Mrs. Ryan, I want you to tell me what happened, in your own words. I know it may be hard, but you can take all of the time you need. Do you mind if I record it?"

"No, I don't mind. Where do you want me to begin?" Cat asked.

"At the beginning," he answered.

"Well, Jim and Mark left and Jim said that he would send someone to protect me while he was gone. He always does that when he has to leave.

"After he had been gone for several hours and no one came, I just assumed that he had forgotten or changed his mind. Really, he never does, though. He always sends someone. So when this man came and told me that Jim had been hurt and was in the hospital, I believed him. He said he would take me to Jim. I never even stopped to question him. I just went with him.

"When he pulled up in front of this building, I said, 'This isn't the hospital. Where are you taking me?' Then he pulled me out of the car, drew a gun on me and forced me into the building. I tried to get away, but he was holding my arm too tightly. Then when I looked over the room, I saw…" Then she paused and tried to hold back the tears.

"Do you need to stop for a minute, Mrs. Ryan?" the Director asked.

"I'll be OK," Cat said, as she choked back her tears. "Just give me a minute."

After Cat regained her composure, she continued. "Jim was tied to a chair and I could see he had been beaten. His face was cut and bleeding and both of his eyes were swollen and bruised. There was a man standing behind him holding a gun on him.

"When Jim saw me, he called my name and told the man to leave me alone. He tried to get loose, but the man behind him hit him with the gun."

Then Cat paused again for a few minutes. "Every time Jim tried to get to me, he hit him again," Cat finally continued "Then the man, they called him Dan, did things to me to make Jim even angrier."

"Things like what?" the Director asked. "Take your time, Mrs. Ryan. I really need you to tell me, if you can. I have to know what possessed Jim to act as he did."

Cat took a deep breath and then slowly continued. "He started to unbutton my blouse and he started kissing me." Then she stopped again.

Thinking that she was finished, the Director asked, "Is that all, Mrs. Ryan?"

"No," Cat answered, then she began again. "When I refused to let him kiss me and tried to pull away from him, he hit me. He tried to kiss me again and, when I refused to kiss him, he kept hitting me. That made Jim so mad, he jumped up, still tied to the chair, and lunged for Dan. Dan hit Jim and, as Jim fell to the floor, I took advantage of the confusion and ran. If Jim hadn't lunged for him when he did, I believe he would have become more violent. He was getting very angry because I was refusing to kiss him. Jim took him by surprise when he lunged at him and I tore loose from his grasp and ran. Jim tripped him, as I headed for the door. I heard him hit Jim again, but I kept on running. I didn't even know if Jim was still alive or not, but I knew he would want me to run and so I did."

Now Cat was crying so hard that Director Halbert could barely make out what she was saying.

"That's OK, Mrs. Ryan," he said. "I can wait until you compose yourself. Would you like some water?"

"Yes, please," she answered.

He poured her a glass from a pitcher on the credenza behind him and handed it to her. He stood beside her and watched until she drank all that she wanted. Then he asked, "What about Agent Mark Fuller? Where was he all during this time?"

"When I was dragged into the room, I saw him lying on the floor with blood oozing from his head. I thought he was dead at first, but later I heard him moan and knew he was only unconscious."

When Cat was calm again, Director Halbert asked, "What happened after Commander Ryan was hit and you escaped?"

"Ben, the other man, ran after me. I hid in a culvert, but I could hear Ben looking for me, so I stayed in the culvert until it started getting dark and I couldn't hear Ben looking for me any longer. I called 911 and tried to give the dispatcher my location, but I didn't really know where I was. Before the police came, Jim had gotten away and had come and found me. He took me to a car where Mark was waiting and Mark drove us home."

"OK, now, is that everything you can remember?" the Director asked.

"Yes, I think so," Cat answered.

"Orretese talked to his lawyer last night and he advised him to take a deal," the Director said. "He said if you will drop the assault charges and Jim will drop the assault and espionage charges, he will drop the charges against Jim. What do you think?"

"I don't know," Cat said. "You'll have to talk to Jim and see what he says."

Director Halbert walked to the door and asked Jim to come into his office. Jim went directly to Cat.

"Are you OK, Hon?" he asked.

"Yes, I'm OK," she answered.

"Sit down, Jim," the Director said. "I have something to ask you. Your wife has given me a good description of the events that led up to your arrest of Orretese. Do you want to hear her version of the incident?"

"I don't need to hear it. I know what she said," Jim answered.

"Are you sure you don't need to hear it?" The Director pressed.

"I know my wife. I know she didn't say anything that isn't true," Jim answered.

"OK, then, I'll go on," the Director continued. "Orretese's lawyer advised him to take a deal. He said he will drop the charges he made against you, if you drop the charges of assault and espionage. What do you say?"

"I say no way," Jim jumped to his feet and shouted. "He repeatedly abused my wife. There's no way I'll let him off."

"Jim, you know if you don't accept his bargain, that I'll have to have you prosecuted don't you? You'll be dismissed, also," Director Halbert said.

"I know," Jim answered with his head lowered.

"Is that what you want?" the Director asked.

"No, you know I don't, but I can't let him get away with attacking my wife either," Jim said.

"Jim," Cat said slowly. "You can't do this. You can't throw away your career and maybe your whole life. I'll eventually get over his abuse and there's still the kidnapping charge, so it won't be like he got away with it. Please, Jim, reconsider."

"Cat, I can't. I just can't," Jim said, as he sat back down and took her hand.

"Do you want a little time to consider it, Jim?" Director Halbert asked. "If you do, I'll give you until tomorrow morning. Then I'll have to do what I have to do. No matter what you decide, I'll have to suspend you. You know what the rules are."

"Yes, Sir, I understand, Sir," Jim answered.

"I'll expect to have your decision in the morning, Director Halbert said. "You two may go now. I'll look for you in the morning."

Jim took Cat's arm and led her out the door. Mark was waiting for them in the waiting room. He got up and followed them out to the car. He opened the door to the back seat for Cat and got into the driver's seat, because Jim had already gotten into the passenger seat and shut the door.

When Mark got into the car, before starting the engine, he asked, "How did it go?"

"Not good," was all Jim said, and Cat remained silent.

When they arrived home, Jim said, "Mark, I've been suspended. You'll have to take over now. You know where everything is. You have a key to my office. You know my passwords. You're all set. I don't need to even go into my office."

"Jim, I don't like this," Mark said. "It's not right."

"Just do as I say, Mark. It'll be better for everyone, if you just do as I say," Jim said, and then he stormed up the stairs and slammed the bedroom door.

"Cat, I'm sorry," Mark said. "I wish there was something I could do."

"Just continue to be his friend," Cat answered. "He really needs a friend right now."

Then she followed Jim up the stairs. She gave a soft knock on the door and said, "Jim, may I come in?"

"Come on in, Cat. I'm not mad at you," he answered. "It's not your fault. It's my own fault. Every bit of it."

"Jim, I love you so much and I can't stand to see you like this," she said, as she sat down on the bed beside him. "Please, just do as Director Halbert said and drop the charges. I'll be all right."

"Maybe you will, but I won't," he said. "I'll never be able to get the thought of his filthy hands on you out of my mind. I'll just have to face the consequences."

"Please, Jim, don't do that," she pleaded. "If you go to prison, I don't know what I'll do. Who'll protect me, then?"

"Just go away and let me think," he finally said. "I need to see what I think I can live with."

That night neither of them slept. When morning finally arrived, they got up, dressed and went downstairs. Neither of them wanted to eat anything, so they just had a cup of coffee and prepared to go.

"Jim, you want me to go with you?" Mark asked.

"No, Mark, we'll do this by ourselves this time," Jim answered.

When they arrived at FSC Headquarters, Director Halbert was waiting for them.

"Come right on in, Jim, Mrs. Ryan," the Director said, as he opened the door to his office and shut it after they entered.

"Sit down," the Director said. "Would you like a cup of coffee?"

"No," they both said in unison.

"Well, have you made your decision?" he asked.

"Yes, I have," Jim said.

"Well, what is it?" the Director asked.

"I'll drop the charges, but only if he drops any and all charges against me," Jim answered.

"Is that your final decision?" the Director asked.

"Yes, Sir, that's my final decision," Jim answered.

"OK, I'll take care of the paperwork," Director Halbert said. "You're still going to have to be suspended for 30 days. Do you understand that?"

"Yes, Sir, I understand," Jim answered.

"Now, the first thing you need to do is take a long vacation with your wife. You need to go somewhere peaceful and quiet where you can relax and recuperate," Director Halbert said.

"Thanks for the suggestion, Sir. I think we'll do that," Jim answered.

"That's all for now. I'll let you know when we need you for Orretese's trial.

"I've put Mark Fuller in charge of my unit while I'm on suspension," Jim said. "The men will follow his orders the same as they would mine."

"I'm glad you did that," the Director said. "You may go now. Send me a postcard. I'd like to know if you're all right." With that, he stood and walked them to the door.

"That wasn't as bad as I thought it would be," Jim said, as he took Cat's arm and led her to their car.

"What do you think about going to Hawaii again?" Jim asked, after he had pulled out onto the highway and headed toward home.

"That sounds great," Cat answered, a little surprised that he would take the Director's suggestion.

"OK, Hawaii it is," he said. Then he drove the rest of the way home in silence.

When they got home, they met with Mark and made plans to take a two-week trip to Hawaii.

"Mark, do you think you'll be OK for two weeks?" Jim asked.

"I don't know, Jim," he answered. "Will you have your cell phone?"

"Not with me. If you run into problems, just figure it out for yourself. You'll have to do that sooner or later anyway," Jim said.

So the next morning, Mark drove Jim and Cat to the airport to catch their flight to Hawaii.

"Now you rest, Jim. I'll take care of everything here. Don't you worry at all," Mark said, as he watched them walk up the ramp to board the plane.

Jim and Cat spent two restful weeks lying on the beach, shopping and sight-seeing. Occasionally, Cat caught Jim pacing the floor with his cell phone in his hand, but he never did make a call.

One morning when Jim awoke, he said, "Cat, I have an idea. Let's go to the shooting range this morning. I'm going to teach you some more ways to defend yourself. I never want you to be at the mercy of a brute like Orretese again."

After breakfast, they headed to the shooting range where Jim instructed Cat on how to shoot different weapons. When she was as proficient with the pistol as he felt she should be, he told her to put it into her purse and always carry it with her.

When they were back at the hotel, they went into the gym and Jim gave Cat another course on self-defense. When he felt that she was able to defend herself, he said, "OK. That's enough. Let's go back to the room, shower and rest for a while."

As they lay on the bed, it occurred to Jim that Cat was ready to join his team now. He turned over and raised up on one elbow. "Cat, how would you like to be a member of my team?"

"I would love it. Do you really mean it?" Cat answered enthusiastically.

"When we get back home, we'll go see about getting you a position on my team," Jim said. "Now, lay down and go to sleep."

She wondered how Jim thought that she could sleep after that, but she closed her eyes and tried. She gave a satisfied sigh, turned over on her side and fell into a comfortable sleep.

When it was time to board the plane for their return trip home, Cat could see a big difference in Jim's appearance. He had a more relaxed look. He even smiled and teased her more. She thought that maybe he was beginning to get back to the old wonderful Jim she had married.

As soon as they landed, though, Jim changed. He became more tense. Everything seemed to bother him. At first, they didn't see Mark with the car.

"Where is he?" Jim wanted to know. "I told him when we would be here. Why isn't he here?"

"Maybe something came up at the last minute," Cat answered. "Just call him and see where he is."

"You call him," Jim said handing her his phone. "I'm afraid of what I might say to him."

"There he is now," Cat said, as she saw Mark rushing toward them.

"I'm sorry, Jim. I couldn't find a parking place. Let me have your luggage," Mark said, as he picked up two of their cases. Jim picked up the other one with one hand and grabbed Cat's arm with the other and followed Mark out the exit.

When they got outside, Mark said, "Wait here and I'll go get the car." While Mark was getting the car, Jim paced back and forth like a caged tiger. When Mark pulled up, Jim could hardly wait for Mark to open the trunk so he could load the luggage into it.

Jim helped Cat into the back seat and then climbed into the front passenger seat.

"Go straight home, Mark," he said. "Don't stop for anything. If Cat needs something, she can get it later."

As soon as Mark pulled up in front of the cabin and stopped, Jim was out and around the car and stood waiting for Mark to open the trunk. He grabbed two cases and headed for the door. Inside the cabin, he didn't wait for Cat or Mark, he just hurried on up the stairs.

"Thanks, Mark," Cat said. "Jim has just gotten like that the closer we were to home. He was doing good while we were in Hawaii. I know he really appreciates what you've done for us. He just can't tell you right now."

"I know, Cat," Mark answered. "Anyway, I'll take this case on up for you and then I have to go take care of some business. I'll be back tonight, though. Oh, I made Jim an appointment with Dr. Richards. He's the Department psychiatrist. It's for Monday, at 10:00 a.m. Do you think he can make it?"

"I'll make sure he does," Cat said. "Will you go with him?"

"Yes, if he'll let me, I'll take him," Mark answered.

When Cat told Jim about the appointment, he just shrugged his shoulders and said, "OK."

That week-end, Jim didn't say much to anyone. He stayed upstairs in their bedroom most of the time. When Monday arrived, he reluctantly dressed and went downstairs. He drank a cup of coffee, but refused to eat anything. The closer it came to time to leave for his appointment, the more tense he became.

"Can I go with you, Jim?" Cat asked, even though she knew what his answer would be.

"No, Cat, you stay here," he answered. "Ted will be here with you. Don't let anyone that you don't know come into this place. No matter what tale they tell you, don't let them come in. Don't you go anywhere with anyone either. Do you understand me?"

"Yes, Jim, I understand," Cat replied.

Then he gave her a quick kiss and followed Mark out the door.

In the doctor's office, Jim refused to sit down. He paced the floor and refused to answer the doctor's questions.

"Jim, you do know why you're here, don't you?" Dr. Richards asked.

"Yes, I know why I'm here," Jim said sarcastically.

"Tell me why you're here, then," Dr. Richards asked.

"I lost it," Jim replied.

"What do you mean, you lost it?" Dr. Richards asked.

"I was supposed to arrest a suspect and instead, I beat him up," Jim answered.

"Tell me, why did you beat him up?" the doctor asked.

"Because he attacked my wife," Jim answered.

"Why did he attack your wife?" Dr. Richards asked, even though he already knew. He had already read a report on Jim that had been sent to him by the Department.

"Because he was trying to make me give him some classified information." Jim said, as he became more agitated.

"Did you give him the information?" Dr. Richards asked.

Jim hesitated before answering. "No, I didn't. Maybe I should have. Then maybe he wouldn't have hit my wife." There was a long pause and then Jim said, "Maybe I should never have married her. I thought I could protect her, but I didn't. It's all my fault. I didn't protect her. I didn't keep my promise. I told her. I promised her I would protect her. I have to leave. That's the only way she'll be safe. I have to leave her."

"Jim, listen to me," Dr. Richards tried to get Jim's attention, but that made him ramble even more.

"I have to leave her. That's the only way to protect her," Jim mumbled.

Then he ran out the door. "Come on, Mark. I'm through," Jim said, as he ran out the exit and to the car.

The secretary called, "Mr. Ryan, I have your next appointment."

"Here, give it to me," Mark said, as he grabbed the appointment card out of her hand and hurried after Jim.

"Jim, what's wrong?" Mark asked when he reached the car.

"Open the car, Mark. Take me home," Jim said angrily.

When Mark had started the car and began moving, he asked again, "Jim, what happened in there? What's wrong?"

"Just shut up and drive me home," Jim said, then wouldn't say another word.

When Mark pulled up in front of the cabin, Jim was out of the car in a flash. He tore through the door and up the stairs and into their bedroom.

"Jim, what's wrong?" Cat asked, as she followed him into the bedroom.

Jim didn't answer. He just grabbed his clothes and carried them down the hall to his old bedroom. Then he came back and gathered the rest of his stuff and carried it to the other room.

"Jim, what are you doing?" Cat asked as she began to cry. "What's wrong? What happened?"

"I'm leaving you, Cat," he said, as he ran back down the stairs and out the back door. "Just leave me the hell alone," he shouted as he slammed the door.

Cat ran down the stairs after him. She was crying so hard now, she could hardly see where she was going.

"What's he doing, Cat?" Mark asked, as he put his arm around her.

"I don't know, Mark. He said he's leaving me." Then she sobbed into Mark's shoulder and he held her and tried to comfort her.

Just then, Jim burst through the back door and saw Cat and Mark together.

"Don't touch her," he yelled. "Get your hands off her." He ran up to Mark and pulled him around and punched him on the chin. "I knew you were doing something behind my back," he said, as he hit him again.

"Jim, stop," Cat cried. "You don't know what you're doing."

"Jim, I was only trying to comfort her," Mark said, trying to get Jim to stop hitting him.

"I know what you were doing," Jim shouted. Then he grabbed his head and said, "Oh, my head," and passed out.

"Jim, Jim, are you all right?" Cat cried. When Jim didn't answer, she said, "Mark, we have to get him to the hospital."

Together, Mark and Ted got Jim into the back seat of the car and Cat climbed in beside him and held his head in her lap. When they got to the hospital, Mark went into the hospital to get someone to bring a gurney out to transport Jim into the Emergency Room.

Jim was taken directly to an examination room and Cat stayed with him while Mark and Ted sat in the waiting room. Jim drifted in and out of consciousness.

Shortly, Dr. Malick came into the room and examined Jim. "Has he had a head injury recently?" he asked.

"Yes," Cat said.

"I'll need to do some blood work and take some X-rays. He also needs a CT scan," the doctor said and then left the room.

Jim opened his eyes and looked at Cat. "Cat, where am I?" he asked.

"You're in the hospital," Cat answered. "You passed out and we brought you here."

"No, Cat, I don't want to be here," he said, as he tried to get up, but he passed out again.

"Oh, Jim," Cat cried. "Don't die. Please don't die." Then she softly cried until the technician came and took him away for X-rays. When the X-ray technician brought him back to the examination room, someone came in and drew blood. Jim didn't even move.

After about three hours, Dr. Malick returned. "Mrs. Ryan, would you come with me for a minute?" he said, as he led her to an alcove just outside the examination room.

"Here are the X-rays of your husband's skull," he explained. "Do you see these dark spots?"

Cat nodded her head.

"That's an intracranial hematoma. It looks as if he has had several head injuries lately. Does he play football?"

"No, he's a Federal Agent," Cat answered. She didn't know if it was all right for her to tell the doctor that, but she thought it might make a difference.

"Anyway," Dr. Malick continued. "These two hematomas or blood clots, if you will, are putting pressure on his brain. Has he been complaining of headaches lately?"

"Well, he does every now and then, but he says it's nothing," Cat answered.

"Has he been acting strange lately?" Dr. Malick continued to question Cat.

"Yes, he has definitely been acting strange," Cat said emphatically.

"I'm going to have to admit him to the hospital as soon as I get a room ready. He will be in Intensive Care. I'll have to keep him in an induced coma until I can schedule surgery. He will have to have surgery to relieve the pressure. I have to keep him sedated. If he wrestles around, he could cause the clot to move. If that happens, well, let's just say we don't want that to happen."

"I need to go talk to someone in the waiting room," Cat said, as she started to cry. "Can I go out and come back in?"

"Sure," he said. "You can bring someone in to be with you if you would like."

When Mark and Ted saw Cat's face and saw how she was crying, they knew it had to be bad.

"What is it, Cat?" Mark asked.

Cat could hardly talk, she was crying so hard. "He has a blood clot on his brain," she said through sniffles. "He has to have surgery. He's going to be in a coma until the surgery."

"When is the surgery?" Mark asked.

"I don't know yet. They're putting him in Intensive Care as soon as they can get a room," she answered.

"Mark, will you go sit in there with me for a while?" she asked.

"Of course I will," Mark answered, then he turned to Ted. "Ted, will you call the guys and let them know what's happening. Also, you need to tell Barbara, our cook. She'll be expecting us. We'll decide what to do about the assignment in the morning. The guys will want to know what to do. Tell them I'll decide in the morning."

When Cat and Mark went back into the room where Jim was, they saw that someone had added an IV to his arm. Dr. Malick met her at the door and asked her to wait for a few minutes.

"We're getting ready to transport him to ICU," he said. "He will be in bed 12. If you'll just step out into the hall for a few minutes until we get him ready to go, then you can go with us."

"I'll go tell Ted that we're going on to ICU," Mark said. "Don't let them leave until I get back."

When Mark got back, they were ready to transport Jim. Cat and Mark followed along as the attendant curved this way and that way until they came to an elevator. The attendant pushed the button and the elevator arrived shortly and they all got onto it.

When they arrived in ICU, Cat and Mark were asked to wait in the waiting room until Jim was ready. When he was ready, a nurse came and took them to Jim's room and let them stay for a few minutes.

Cat's heart sank when she saw Jim. There was an IV pole with several bags hanging from it and he had an oxygen mask on his face, which was as pale as the pillow case his head was lying on. Cat started to cry and Mark put an arm around her shoulders. "Maybe it's not as bad as it looks," he said softly.

"I can't stand to see him like that," she said, as she tried to touch his arm. He never even moved when she called his name.

"The doctor said he would be sedated, Cat," Mark said.

"I know, but I just want him to know that I'm here, if he can hear me," she said through her tears.

Soon, the nurse asked them to leave. "You can see him again at the regular visiting time," she said, as she led them back out. "I will need your cell phone number."

"Here it is, but I'm going to stay here," Cat answered.

"That's OK, but I need to be able to get in touch with you no matter where you are, in case of an emergency," she said.

Then Cat and Mark went back to the waiting room. Ted was already there waiting for them. He and Mark walked out into the hall to discuss what to do about their assignment. Cat sat down and tried to look at a magazine and take her mind off Jim's condition.

Soon, Mark and Ted returned. "I'm sending Ted home to get some things we'll need," Mark said. "Will you make a list of what you need so he can bring them back?"

"Oh, yes, thank you. I didn't even think about that," Cat said, as she dug into her purse for a pen and paper. After trying to think of everything she would need, she handed the list to Mark.

"Here, Ted," Mark said, as he handed the list to Ted. "Bring this back to us and then you can go back and stay at Jim's place until in the morning."

The waiting room attendant then took Cat and Mark to another little room. "Wait here and Dr. Johnson will come and talk to you," she said.

Shortly, a tall, slim man with graying hair came into the room and introduced himself as Dr. Rick Johnson.

"You are Mrs. Ryan, I assume?" he started.

"Yes, I am, and this is Jim's best friend, Mark Fuller," Cat answered.

"You have been informed as to your husband's condition?" he asked.

"Yes, Dr. Malick showed me some X-rays and said he had a blood clot on his brain," Cat answered.

"Yes, well, I have scheduled surgery for 9:00 in the morning. Will that give you time to notify your family?"

"Yes, Dr. Johnson," Cat answered breathlessly.

Then Dr. Johnson opened a booklet that he was carrying and described the procedure that he would follow to relieve the pressure that the blood clot was putting on Jim's brain.

"After the surgery, it will take a few months for him to get back to the normal use of his brain," Dr. Johnson explained. "At first, when we get him up, he will lack coordination. When he tries to walk, he will veer to the left or right. It will be difficult for him to walk straight. He will probably run into the wall a lot. He will be very frustrated, I'm sure. Most patients, who have had this surgery, get very frustrated, so don't be alarmed when he does get agitated. Some women almost divorce their husbands after this type of surgery.

"We'll keep him sedated at first, because we don't want him thrashing around. That should just take a few days. Then we'll gradually awaken him and start getting him up. It will be a long process. I just want you to realize what is facing you. Do you have any questions?"

"Will Jim be all right afterward?" Cat asked. "I mean will he be himself?"

"I'm sorry, Mrs. Ryan, I can't answer that," Dr. Johnson said. "We'll just have to wait and see. Some patients bounce right back with no aftereffects and some don't do so well. It all depends on how much damage has been done to his brain and how determined he is to get well. Is there anything else you want to know?"

"No, I guess not," Cat answered. "Mark, do you want to ask anything?"

"No, Cat," Mark answered. "I understand what Dr. Johnson said. It looks like a long and difficult road ahead."

"If there isn't anything else, I'll leave this pamphlet with you.

You may want to read it again. My office phone number is there if you need to ask me anything else. I'll be here first thing in the morning. I'll come and talk to you after the surgery, which will probably take about five or six hours and probably another hour in recovery, depending on how he does. Bye for now," Dr. Johnson said, then he left.

When he was gone, Cat began to cry again. Mark put his arm around her shoulders to comfort her.

"Oh, Mark, what will I do if he doesn't make it?" she sobbed.

"Don't even think about that, Cat. Just pray that God will take care of him and believe that He will," Mark said. "I know, if anyone can make it through this, Jim will. Just remember, I'm always here for you." He wanted to add, "I'll always love and protect you," but he decided that it was best if he didn't say that right now. He might regret saying that later on when Jim was well.

Mark's confidence strengthened Cat and she stopped crying and began to pray. Afterward, she began to feel that everything was going to be all right.

"I need to call Carol and Charlotte," Cat said. "Let me do that before I go back into the waiting room."

"Carol," Cat said when Carol answered the phone. Cat was crying so hard that Carol wasn't sure it was Cat.

"Cat, is that you? What's wrong?" Carol asked, becoming frightened.

"Carol, it's Jim," Cat finally got out. "Jim's going to have to have brain surgery in the morning."

"What?" Carol asked. "What do you mean brain surgery?"

Then Cat explained to Carol about the blood clot and that Jim's surgery was scheduled for 9:00 in the morning.

"I'll tell Skip and we'll leave as soon as we can," Carol answered. "I'll see you sometime tonight. We may just come on to the hospital without going by the cabin. We'll get there as soon as we can."

After talking to Carol, Cat dialed Charlotte's number and hoped that she wasn't in the middle of filming.

"Charlotte," Cat said when Charlotte answered the phone. "Jim is in really bad shape. He's going to have brain surgery in the morning."

"Oh, Cat, I'm so sorry," Charlotte said. "We're just about to break for the holidays. I'll just tell them I have to leave early. I'll see if I can get a flight out this afternoon. I'll tell Tyler and we'll get there as soon as we can."

Cat was thankful that she and Charlotte were now on good terms. She really would like for her to get there in time for Jim's surgery.

After she made her calls, she and Mark returned to the large waiting room and informed the attendant that they would be there if they were needed.

Ted had brought their things and decided to stay a while to see how Jim was doing. He and Mark went to an obscure corner and discussed again what to do about their latest assignment. It was going to be hard enough without Jim, but even harder without Jim and Mark.

About 9:00 p.m., Carol and Skip arrived. Carol and Cat hugged and cried while Skip talked to Mark. Shortly after they arrived, Charlotte and Tyler arrived. The hugging and crying were repeated with Charlotte.

Cat and Mark then tried to fill the new arrivals in on what had been happening. At 10:00 p.m., the last visiting time was announced for the patients in ICU. Only two visitors per patient were allowed to go at one time, so Cat and Mark went first.

Jim was still asleep and looked even paler than he had been when they saw him before. When Cat touched his arm and called his name, he didn't even flinch. "I love you, Jim," she whispered, hoping that somehow her words might penetrate the heavy cloak with which Jim was covered by the sedative.

"I'll go back and let either Carol or Charlotte come in," Mark said. "You just stay here with Jim until the visiting time is over."

Carol, Charlotte, Tyler, Skip and then Ted took turns coming into the room for a few minutes. They took one look at Jim and left. Carol and Charlotte left in tears and the men left with a sad look on their faces.

When the visiting time was over, Mark went back to escort Cat back into the waiting room. Cat caressed Jim's face and arm and again said, "Jim, I love you," and reluctantly walked out with Mark.

Back in the waiting room, Carol and Charlotte were trying to decide whether to go to Jim's cabin or their cabin.

"I think we should go to our cabin," Carol said. "That way it would leave room in Jim's cabin for some of Jim's team who might want to stay."

"That's OK with us," Charlotte said. "Is it ready for occupation?"

"It should be," Cat answered. "I asked Molly to get someone to change the beds and clean the cabin because I knew that Carol and Skip would be coming home for Thanksgiving soon."

"Do you realize what else is coming soon?" Carol asked.

"Yes, our one-year anniversary," Cat said and began to cry again. "I don't know if Jim will even remember."

"Surely he'll remember that," Carol said.

"The doctor said that it would be a while before he would remember things," Cat answered.

"Well, I'm sure he'll remember that," Carol said again, trying to encourage Cat.

Since the arrangements had been decided, Carol and Charlotte hugged and kissed Cat and said they would see her in the morning. They said they were really tired and needed to get settled before going to bed, since they would have to be up so early in the morning.

Since Charlotte and Tyler had taken a taxi from the airport to the hospital, they rode with Skip and Carol to their cabin. Ted said that he would go with them to make sure everything was OK in the cabin. He and Mark decided to wait until after Jim's surgery before starting on their new assignment.

After everyone left, Cat sat down in one of the recliners in the waiting room and softly cried. Mark had walked Ted and the others to the elevator and had returned to the waiting room. He took Cat's hands and pulled her into his arms. "Come on, Cat," he said handing her a tissue. "Dry your eyes and have a little faith. God will take care of Jim. I know He will. Did you call Rev. Miller and tell him about Jim's surgery?"

"Yes, I did. He said he'd be here in the morning," Cat replied.

Then Mark kissed Cat's cheek and sat her back down in the recliner. He patted her arm and sat down in the recliner next to her. "I think I'll try to get some sleep," he said. "It's been a long day and it'll be a long day tomorrow. Why don't you try to get some sleep, too?"

"I'll try," Cat said, but no matter how hard she tried, she was still awake when people started arriving the next morning.

Just before 8:00 a.m., Carol, Skip, Charlotte, Tyler and Ted arrived. The attendant came and talked to Cat about Jim's surgery. She informed Cat that the surgery would take approximately six hours, but someone would call and let her know how things were going at intervals during that time. Cat told her that she and Mark would be there the whole time if anyone needed them. Then they all sat down and prepared to wait for word about Jim.

Soon Rev. Miller arrived and had a prayer with them. That made Cat feel a lot better, even though she and Mark had been praying most of the night.

About 9:00, someone called to tell Cat that Jim's surgery had begun and, as the attendant had said, someone called occasionally to tell Cat that everything was going well.

About 11:00 a.m., someone suggested that they all go to the cafeteria for lunch, since no one had taken time for breakfast.

"You all go on," Cat said. "I'll just wait here. I'm not really hungry anyway."

Some of them decided to go while they had the chance, but Mark said he was staying with Cat. Every now and then, some of Jim's team members dropped by to see how he was doing and Mark and Ted would fill them in on his progress.

About 2:00 p.m., the attendant said that Dr. Johnson wanted to talk to Cat, so she and Mark followed her into the small room again. When Dr. Johnson came into the room, he sat in a chair in front of Cat and Mark.

"Mrs. Ryan," he began. "Everything went well. I removed the clot and released the pressure. I can already see a definite change in Mr. Ryan's brain cells. We won't know how successful the operation was until later when he is awake and his ability can be evaluated. That will depend on the amount of damage to his brain cells.

"We will keep him sedated for several days. I don't want him thrashing around, as I told you yesterday. His memory will be spotty at first. He will be frustrated, because he will not be able to remember much that happened before the surgery.

"We'll get him up slowly in about a week and see how he walks. As I told you before, he will have to learn to walk all over again. That will frustrate him. His hands probably will not work like he wants them to work. You will need to be patient with him and show him that he is still the man you love, no matter what. Some men can't stand to be an invalid. If his brain cells are damaged too much, you'll have to expect that. I want to really stress to you that you will need to be patient with him. Do you understand?"

"Yes, Doctor Johnson, I think I understand what you're trying to say," Cat answered.

"You, best friend," Dr. Johnson turned his attention to Mark. "You will need to really be a good friend. He'll need someone to talk to. You'll need to be that one."

"Yes, Sir," Mark answered. "I'll be there for him. He's always been there for me."

"Good. Now, do either of you have any more questions?"

"How soon can I see him?" Cat asked.

"Give it a couple of hours," he answered. "Remember, he'll be sedated. He won't even know you're there. Now, anything else?"

"No, I don't have anything else. Do you, Mark?" Cat answered.

"No," Mark answered.

"I'll leave an appointment and prescriptions for him when he goes home, which probably won't be until next week. I'll also check on him each day until he goes home. If that's all, I'll see you later."

They both nodded and Dr. Johnson left.

After a couple of hours, Cat was notified that they could go in and see Jim for a few minutes. When Cat walked up to Jim's bed, she started to cry again. Jim looked terrible. There was a large bandage that covered most of the top of his head. There were wires attached to him and then attached to a machine that clicked constantly. There was the usual IV pole with several bottles with solution that ran down a tube into his arm and he was even paler than he had been. His eyes were closed and he never even moved at all when she touched him.

After watching her stand by Jim's bed and cry, Mark put his arm around her shoulders and kissed her cheek and then he kissed her forehead and held her to his chest. Then he said, "Come on, Cat, he doesn't even know you're here. Let's go back to the waiting room."

When they returned to the waiting room, all the others had returned from the cafeteria and were waiting to hear how he was doing.

"Is it over?" Charlotte asked.

"Yes, we just got to see him for a minute," Cat answered.

"How's he doing?" Carol wanted to know.

"The doctor said he's doing good, but he doesn't look good," Cat answered. "He looks terrible."

"Can we go see him?" Carol asked.

"I don't know. You need to ask the attendant," Cat answered. "You'll regret it, though. I don't think you want to see him like that."

"Maybe we'll wait until the next visiting time, then," she said.

Rev. Miller had been waiting for Cat to return. When he saw her and Mark come back, he said, "Cat, I'd like to go have a prayer for Jim. Will you and Mark come back with me?"

"Yes, if they'll let us go back again," Cat answered.

"I'm sure they will," he said, as he led them back to Jim's room.

They held hands and circled around Jim's bed. They bowed their heads, as Rev. Miller prayed for a speedy recovery for Jim. After he said, "Amen," he walked with them out into the hall.

"I'm going now, Cat," he said. "You have my number, if you need me. I'll be back to check on him, but you call me if he gets worse and I'll be right here."

"Thank you, Rev. Miller," Cat said, as she took his offered hand. "I appreciate your being here. You really helped me make it through it."

"See you later," he said and ran to catch the elevator.

"Well, are you ready to go back to the waiting room?" Mark asked.

"Let's wait just a few minutes," Cat answered. "I just need a minute to get control of myself. I know God will take care of him, but I'm so afraid that he'll never be himself again. Oh, Mark, what will I do if he's still like he was before we came to the hospital?" Then she began to cry again.

"He won't be, Cat," Mark said, as he held her to his chest and let her cry. Then he put his hand under her chin, tilted her lips up to his and kissed her tenderly. "He won't be, Cat. I know he won't be," he said.

CHAPTER 4

On the third day, they began bringing Jim out of his induced coma. Cat sat in his room waiting for him to open his eyes. Slowly, he opened them and looked around. "Cat," he said when he saw her. "Cat, where am I? What's going on?" She could see that he was becoming agitated, so she rushed over to his side and grabbed his hand.

"You're in the hospital, Jim. You've had some serious surgery," she said.

"What do you mean?" he asked, as he felt the bandage on his head and pulled at the IV line. "What's all this?"

"I told you, Jim" she answered. "You've had surgery."

"Why?" he asked.

"You had a blood clot on your brain and you passed out," she answered, as she held his hand to keep him from pulling at the IV. "Mark and I had to bring you to the hospital."

"I don't remember," Jim looked confused. "When did you bring me here? Oh, my head hurts. What's this?" he said, as he pulled at the bandage.

Cat pushed the call button for the nurse because Jim was becoming more and more agitated.

Mark had just gone out to the waiting room to see Ted and some of the other team members and saw the nurse rush into Jim's room, as he was returning. He hurried to the room to see what was happening. When he saw the nurse trying to calm Jim down and Cat crying, he hurried to Cat.

"He's confused and very agitated," Cat told Mark.

When the nurse finally put a shot into the IV line, Jim finally closed his eyes and calmed down.

"What happened?" Mark asked.

"He wanted to know where he was and why," Cat whispered. "When I told him, he became very agitated."

"Come on, Cat," Mark said. "Let's go back out to the waiting room and let that shot do its thing." Then he led her back out to the waiting room where Carol and Charlotte were waiting.

"How is he today?" they asked.

"Not good," Cat answered. "They started waking him up and he became very agitated. I can't stand to see him like that."

The next day, the doctor began bringing him out a little more and started having him sit on the side of the bed. When he was able to sit up by himself on the side of the bed, he was transferred to the "Step Down" unit, where he would begin coming back even more. He would have a private room and Cat and Mark would be able to stay with him all of the time.

The next morning, when he opened his eyes, Cat was standing next to the bed. He looked up at her and said, "Cat, where am I?"

"You're in the hospital, Jim," she answered.

"Why?" he asked.

"You've had to have surgery," she answered.

"Why? What is all this?" he asked again.

"You had a blood clot and the doctor said you had to have surgery," Cat answered.

"I don't remember. What happened?" Jim was becoming agitated again.

"Jim, please calm down," Cat said and tried to take his hand, but he pulled it away and pulled at his IV line again.

"Help me, Cat. Help me get out of this," he pleaded.

"No, Jim, you have to have that. You've had surgery," Cat said, as she still tried to calm him down. Then Mark came over and tried to hold his other hand.

"Mark, what are you doing?" Jim asked. "Let go of me. I have to get this off."

The next day was better. Cat got on one side of Jim and Mark on the other and they walked him down the hall a short way. Then they walked him back to his room. They only gave him pain medicine when he asked for it, but he was still very confused.

"Cat, I can't remember anything," he told her. "Why can't I remember? I don't remember coming to the hospital. I don't remember anything about the surgery. Why can't I remember?"

"You were unconscious when we brought you here, so that's why you don't remember coming here," Cat answered.

"I've tried and I don't remember anything since we came back from our honeymoon," he said. "We did get married didn't we?"

"Yes, Jim, we got married and had a wonderful honeymoon," Cat smiled, as she remembered the wonderful wedding and honeymoon.

"My head hurts when I try to remember," Jim said holding his head.

"Don't try to remember so hard. It'll come back eventually," Cat said.

Each day, Jim walked a little farther down the hall with Cat on one side and Mark on the other. Then one day, he said, "Let me try by myself. Walk with me, but don't help me."

Just as Dr. Johnson said, he couldn't walk straight. He kept walking into the wall, but he was determined to walk by himself. Cat was so happy to see his determination. She finally felt like the old Jim was coming back to her.

The next day, when Dr. Johnson came in to check on Jim, he asked, "How would you like to go home tomorrow, Jim?"

"I would love to go home," Jim answered.

"You've really improved these last two days. I'm sending you home, but you'll need to come back for a while for therapy. Are you willing to do that?"

"Yes, anything to get out of this place," Jim answered.

"OK, I'll discharge you in the morning. I'll leave an appointment and some prescriptions for you. I want to see you next week in my office."

With that, he walked out and Jim said, "I'm ready to go home. How about you, Cat?"

"Yes, I'm ready, too," she answered and silently thanked God.

That night, as they were walking down the hall, Jim saw the Thanksgiving Day decorations that were being put up.

"Cat, what day is today?" he asked.

"It's Monday," Cat answered.

"I mean what day?" he asked again.

"It's November 10, why?" she asked.

"It's almost Thanksgiving isn't it? he asked.

"Yes, that's why Carol and Charlotte were able to come while you were in the hospital," she answered.

Cat didn't mention that their anniversary was also getting close. She didn't want him to get agitated if he couldn't remember it.

The next morning, the nurse came into Jim's room to discharge him. As she was filling out the papers, Jim said, "Mark, go get the car."

"I will, Jim. When she finishes and you're ready to go," Mark answered.

"Go now, Mark. I said go get the car now. I don't want to be standing down there waiting for you to come."

"Sure, Jim," Mark said, as he walked toward the door. "I'll go right now."

The nurse helped Jim into a wheelchair and wheeled him out of the room and into the elevator. When Jim, Cat and the nurse arrived at the front entrance, Mark was there waiting for them with the car parked right in front.

"Do you want to sit up front or in back with Cat?" Mark asked, as he opened both doors.

"I'll sit in back with my wife," he said and got into the car and fastened his seat belt. Cat got in the other side and started to fasten her seat belt, but Jim grabbed her arm and pulled her over to him. "Sit here," he said. "Use this seat belt."

"OK, Jim," Cat said, as she pulled the middle seat belt out and fastened it.

"Mark, take me straight home. Don't stop anywhere," Jim said, as Mark started the car and pulled away from the curb.

"What about your medicine? The doctor gave you some prescriptions." Mark said.

"You can get them later. Just take me home now." Jim was beginning to get agitated again.

When Mark pulled up in front of the cabin, Jim got out and walked to the back of the car to wait for Mark to open the trunk.

"I'll get those, Jim," Mark said, as he opened the trunk. "You just go on into the cabin." Jim turned and walked up to the door and stopped. He just looked at the door and waited for someone to open it for him.

Cat ran up the stairs and opened the door and Jim walked in before her.

He walked straight to his office door and stopped. "Where's my key?" he asked.

Mark set down the cases he was carrying and hurried over to the door and unlocked it. "There you are," Mark said, as he opened the door. Jim stood at the door and looked around his office. "You changed things," he said.

"Yeah, I fixed it so it would be handier for me," Mark hoped that that would satisfy Jim.

Jim then went over to his chair behind his desk and typed his password into the computer. It immediately came on. "Well, I can still get into my computer," he said sarcastically.

"Jim, I had to keep the unit going," Mark started to explain.

"I know, Mark," Jim said slowly. "Am I suspended?" he asked. "I somehow remember being suspended."

"You have two more weeks to go," Mark answered.

"Well, at least you're being honest with me. I guess you took care of Cat, too," Jim said, still with sarcasm.

"Jim, I didn't want to take your job," Mark started, but Jim cut him off.

"Stop, Mark," he said. "I know you did what you had to do. Dang, I wish I could remember everything. Shut the door."

Mark turned around and closed the door.

"Tell me, Mark," Jim pleaded. "Tell me everything. I've got to know. How did I get the blood clot? What happened to me? Tell me."

Mark took a deep breath and said, "Jim, you're not well enough yet. You'll remember on your own eventually."

Jim slammed his fist down on the desk and raised his voice, "Mark, I said tell me, now. I can't wait another day. Why was I suspended?"

"OK, Jim, you win. I'll tell you, but you won't be happy when I get through," Mark answered.

"I'm not happy now, Mark. Can't you see that?" Jim raised his voice again.

"OK, Jim, do you remember Orretese?"

"Orretese, yeah, he was selling classified information to ISIS," Jim said.

"Well, we discovered where he was staying and went to arrest him. Someone tipped him off and he was ready for us. He got us. He had you tied to a chair, beating you to a pulp and I was knocked out. We managed to escape, but you were determined to arrest him.

"Several weeks later, we found out again where he was. You got the team to back us up and we arrested him. You weren't satisfied with just arresting him, you beat him until he passed out.

"When we got him to headquarters, he complained that you used excessive force on him. The cuts and bruises on his face proved he was telling the truth. So you were suspended."

"There's something you're not telling me. I've never beat up a prisoner like that. Why did I do it this time?" Jim was confused.

"I don't know, Jim. I tried to stop you, but you wouldn't listen to me," Mark said.

"Tell me the truth, Mark. What did you leave out? Tell me," Jim was getting agitated again.

"Jim, that's it," Mark said, trying to calm him down. "Now, come on, you've had a rough day. Come on and lie down on the sofa in the den and rest."

Jim slowly logged off of the computer, rose and walked to the door of his office. "I'm going to remember one day, Mark, and when I do, you'll regret not telling me."

"And you may regret remembering," Mark mumbled under his breath. He thought that Jim was far enough ahead of him that he didn't hear, but he heard.

"Where do you want his stuff?" Mark asked Cat, as he walked into the den.

"Put it in our bedroom. Would you also get his clothes and other things and put them back into our bedroom?" Cat asked quietly, so that Jim didn't hear her.

"Sure, Cat," Mark said, as he picked up the cases and headed up the stairs.

Jim lay down on the sofa in the den and called Cat. "Hon, will you come here a minute?"

Cat hurried over to see what Jim wanted. He pulled her down to him and kissed her. "I love you, Cat. More than anything else in the world. Do you still love me?"

"Yes, Jim. You know I do," she answered.

"No, Cat. I don't know for sure. Do you still love me after all I've done?"

"Jim, I don't think you could do anything that would make me stop loving you. I might be disappointed in you sometimes, but I would never stop loving you."

"I think I'm remembering things that I don't want to remember. Maybe I'm blocking them out. I don't know. How will I be when

I remember everything? What kind of person will I be? Will you even like me then?"

"Jim, I will always love you," she leaned down and kissed him. "Now, you go to sleep and rest for a while. You'll feel better after you rest."

That night, with Mark's and Cat's help, Jim went into the bedroom he shared with Cat. It didn't seem as though he remembered removing his things. He just automatically undressed and got into bed as usual. Cat was glad about that. She was afraid that he would remember how he had stormed out with his clothes. She shouldn't have worried, though. That was another thing that had been pushed out of his memory.

That night, they made love. Cat was so happy. She felt like Jim was finally on the road to recovery. She said a prayer of thankfulness to God for finally beginning Jim's healing process.

Mark and Ted went back to taking over Jim's duties as Unit Commander of Jim's FS Unit. Jim quietly watched from the den. He didn't attempt to go into his office again. He went to his therapy when he had to go. If Mark or Ted couldn't take him, one of the other team members would take him.

Then it was the day of his appointment with Dr. Johnson. He was nervous about going to see him for some reason. Mark left Ted in charge of the unit and drove Cat and Jim to Dr. Johnson's office. He waited in the waiting room while Cat and Jim went in to see the doctor.

Dr. Johnson examined Jim's wound, and said it was healing nicely. He had Jim walk across the floor to see if he was walking straighter. He was. He gave him three words to remember and asked him later to repeat them. He did.

Then Dr. Johnson said, "Mrs. Ryan, you can help Jim's memory by reminding him of certain things. Ask him his favorite color; his favorite food; did he have a favorite pet or song. You can think of things that will jog his memory. This will help him get back to reality. The more he remembers of the past, the better he will be at coping with the present."

When Dr. Johnson finished his examination of Jim, he said, "Well, Jim, I think you're well on your way to recovery. I would like to see you again in three months. You can make an appointment as you go out." Then he walked them to the door. Jim stopped at the door and said, "Cat, you go on out. I want to talk to the doctor a minute." Then he pushed her on out the door and shut it.

"Doc, I need to know," Jim began, "Will I ever be myself again? What kind of person will I be? When I remember things, how will it affect me? I really need to know."

"Jim," Dr. Johnson said. "I don't know. Some patients go back to being the same as they were before and some never do. It all depends on the person and how strong their character is. You'll just have to take one day at a time."

"Thanks, Doc. I just thought you could tell me in advance," Jim said slowly and turned and walked out into the waiting room where Cat and Mark were waiting for him. This time, Jim opened the door for Cat to get into the back seat. Then he got into the front seat with Mark. He took an interest in the traffic and how Mark was driving. "Yes," thought Cat. "He's coming back."

CHAPTER 5

When they arrived back at the cabin after Jim's appointment with Dr. Johnson, Mark went into Jim's office and Jim followed him. "I may be suspended, but I can still observe can't I?" Jim asked.

"Sure, Jim," Mark answered. "You can do more than observe. You can offer advice, too."

"I probably won't do that," Jim answered. "You seem to be doing a good job."

After Jim sat silently for a while, he asked, "Mark, what do you think about Cat?"

"What do you mean?" Mark asked cautiously. He didn't like how this was going.

"I mean just that. What do you think of Cat?" Jim asked again.

"I think she's a great lady," Mark answered. "I think you're lucky to have her."

"Do you love her?" Jim asked.

"All right, Jim." Mark stopped what he had been doing on the computer and walked over to face Jim.

"I don't like what you're insinuating," Mark said. "She's your wife and I respect that. I am loyal to you even if you don't realize that. I know before your surgery, you had that idea, but I thought maybe that was the illness. Even if I did want her, I know I wouldn't have a chance in hell. She's crazy about you, Jim. Don't you know that?"

"I'm sorry, Mark," Jim held his head in his hands. "I just don't know if I'll ever be back to myself. I don't even like myself any more, how can she still love me? How can you even like me any more?"

Mark put his hand on Jim's shoulder and said, "Jim, Cat and I both love you. You're like a brother to me. You're my best friend. I would never do anything to deliberately hurt you, and I feel that Cat is the same way. Yes, I love her. I'll admit that, but she's your wife. I know where my boundaries are. You can trust me. I will never dishonor that trust."

"Thank you, Mark, for being honest with me," Jim said, as he rose and opened the door. "I think I'll go upstairs and rest now."

When Cat saw Jim, she wondered what had happened in his office. He looked so depressed. Maybe it was the thought that Mark was doing the job he was supposed to be doing. She followed him up the stairs and sat down beside him on the bed.

"What's wrong, Jim?" she asked.

"Cat, do you still love me?" he asked.

"Of course I do, Jim. I've already told you that," she answered. "I'll never stop loving you. Why do you ask?"

"How do you feel about Mark?" Jim asked.

"What do you mean?" Cat asked.

"I want to know how you feel about Mark? Do you love him?"

"Of course, I love him," she said. "He's like one of our family. He always watches out for us. He's your best friend. Why shouldn't I love him?"

"I mean do you love him?" Jim asked accenting each word.

"Jim, I know what you're getting at and I say stop it. I'm your wife. I love you and I have loved you ever since I was 12 years old. I could never love anyone else like I love you. Your illness is making you think like that, so forget it. I would never cheat on you. No matter how sick you may be. One of our marriage vows said I would stand by you in sickness and I will always honor that vow," Cat said.

Then Jim pulled her to him and kissed her. "I'm sorry, Cat. I had to know. I can't help how I feel. Maybe some day, I'll be well and I'll like myself again, but now I don't and I guess I can't see how you or anyone else can even like me, much less love me."

"I do love you, Jim," Cat said. "I love you more than I could ever love anyone else."

"Thanks, Cat," Jim said, as he lay down on the bed again. "I think I'll rest now."

Then he closed his eyes and Cat went back downstairs.

The day for his appearance before the review board arrived and Mark drove him to headquarters. Cat wanted to go with him, but he refused to let her go. His memory of the Orretese incident was like Swiss Cheese; it was full of holes.

"How am I going to answer their questions if I can't remember anything, Mark?" Jim asked.

"Maybe that's the best thing for you, Jim," Mark answered. "Just do the best you can and let them be the judge."

Jim and Mark sat in the waiting room until the commissioners were ready to see him. When they called his name, Jim nervously walked into the board room. Mark walked in behind him and took a seat.

Jim was asked to tell them what happened. He turned to Mark and expected him to tell what had happened.

"Commander Ryan, we want your version of what happened, not Agent Fuller's version."

"I don't remember what happened, Sir," Jim answered.

"I see from your record that you have had surgery and are under a doctor's care," the Commissioner said. "Is this why you don't remember?"

"Yes, Sir," Jim answered. "All I remember is that Mark, Agent Fuller, and I went to arrest Orretese and we were taken prisoner. We were both beaten. I don't remember anything after that. I know that we escaped our captors, but I don't remember how, and I hardly remember anything until I woke up in the hospital with tubes everywhere and I hurt like hell."

"That's all you remember, then?" the Commissioner asked.

"Yes, Sir. That's all I remember," Jim answered.

"You may step out into the waiting area now while we make our decision," the Commissioner said.

When Mark stood and started to follow Jim, the Commissioner said, "Agent Fuller stay for a minute. We want to ask you a question or two."

"Yes, Sir," he said, as he watched Jim walk out and close the door.

"You are very close to Commander Ryan I'm told. Are you not?" the Commissioner began.

"Yes, Sir, I am," Mark answered.

"You would do anything for him, I suppose," the Commissioner asked.

"Yes, Sir, I would," Mark answered without hesitation.

"Even lie for him?" the Commissioner asked.

"No, Sir. He knows I wouldn't lie for him and he wouldn't expect me to," Mark answered quickly.

"Then, how do you explain your answer to the booking agent when he asked why Orretese was so badly beaten?" the Commissioner asked.

"I said that Orretese resisted arrest, which he did, Sir," Mark answered.

"How did he resist arrest?" the Commissioner asked.

"He hit Commander Ryan, Sir," Mark answered.

"When did he hit Commander Ryan?" the Commissioner persisted.

"After Commander Ryan told him to hit him," Mark sighed.

"So, now we know the truth. Commander Ryan provoked Orretese, didn't he?" the Commissioner asked.

"Yes, Sir," was all Mark could say.

"Thank you, Agent Fuller. That will be all. Now we can make our decision," the Commissioner answered. Mark walked to the door with his head bowed. He knew he had messed up, but what could he do?

Jim was expectantly waiting for Mark when he walked out of the board room.

"Well, how did it go?" Jim asked.

"Not good," Mark answered.

"What happens now?" Jim asked.

"I don't know. I guess we sit and wait," Mark answered.

After about an hour, Jim and Mark were called back into the board room.

"Commander Ryan, the Board has made its decision," the Commissioner began. "After studying your record, we find it completely without a blemish of any kind. We also understand that the hematoma that caused your medical problems was caused by Mr. Orretese and it also prevents you from defending your actions, because of your memory loss. We also feel that, had it not been for your medical problem, you would never have used excessive force on Mr. Orretese. Therefore, it is the unanimous decision of the Board to reinstate you to your previous position of authority."

Jim almost shouted, but he remained silent and turned around to give Mark a broad smile.

"The board also feels that you are not ready to fill that position of authority yet, due to your medical condition. We want to put you on Medical Leave until the first of the year. By then, you should be well enough to perform your duties.

"We also recommend that Agent Mark Fuller be given your position of authority until you are able to perform your duties. You will, of course, remain an advisor at such times when Agent Fuller deems it necessary. You will, of course, receive your usual salary during this time. Do you have any questions?" the Commissioner asked.

"No, Sir. I think you covered everything," Jim answered. "One thing I would like to make sure of, though. I will be allowed to accompany my team on missions to observe will I not?"

"Yes, of course," the Commissioner answered. "Just remain an observer and don't participate until you have fully recovered. At that time, you'll be examined and it will be determined whether you're ready for active duty or not."

"Thank you, Sir," Jim said. "I appreciate your decision."

As Jim and Mark walked out the door of the boardroom, Jim said, "Boy, was I dreading that. I had no idea what I was going to say. I can hardly believe it worked out so well."

"God answers prayers, Jim," Mark said. "You've had a lot of them going up for you."

"I know, Mark, and I appreciate every one of them," Jim answered. "I'm sorry that I've been so difficult lately. I'll try to be better. You're really a good friend and I shouldn't have even thought that you would do anything to betray me. I've been mean to Cat, too. That, I will regret the rest of my life."

"I know, Jim," Mark said. "I understand what caused it. Let's just forget you even said what you said. It's Cat you need to apologize to."

"I did apologize to her," Jim answered. "Now I have to make it up to her. Our anniversary is coming up, I guess you know. Take me by the jeweler's. I need to get her something nice for our anniversary."

At the jeweler's, Jim picked out a gaudy, expensive necklace with a lot of diamonds in it. "What about this, Mark? Do you think she'd like this?"

"No, Jim, I don't," Mark said, as he picked up a simple little heart-shaped necklace that was as delicate and fragile as a butterfly's wing. "Don't you even know your own wife? This is more like what she would like," Mark said, as he held it up for Jim to see.

"You're right, Mark. I guess you know my wife better than I do. Of course she would like a delicate, little thing like that better than a gaudy thing like this," Jim said, as he put down the gaudy one and took the delicate one out of Mark's hand and examined it.

"Yes, she'd love this one. Thank you again for the help," Jim said.

Jim bought the heart-shaped necklace and asked them to gift wrap it for him. Then he told Mark he was ready to go home. When they arrived at the cabin, Jim jumped out of the car and hurried into the cabin. "Cat," he called. "Cat, where are you?"

She came out of the kitchen and said, "Here I am, Jim. How did it go?"

"It went great," he said, as he grabbed her and danced around the room with her. "They reinstated me, but they put me on Medical Leave until the new year. I still have my job. They made Mark the Acting Commander until I'm able to command again. They said I can go on missions as an observer. Isn't that great?"

"Yes, Jim," she said not as enthusiastically as he did. "That's great."

"Now, if I can just get my memory back, I'll be all set," he said, as he grabbed her around the waist and kissed her hard.

"Dr. Johnson said to ask you things that would help your memory," Cat said. "What is your favorite color?"

"Blue, my dear," he answered. "Blue like the dress you were wearing the day I discovered that I was deeply in love with you."

"What dress?" Cat asked.

"You know the one. The one with the lace and the V neck. The one that shows your great figure," Jim said and he slapped her on the bottom.

"Jim, don't do that. Mark's standing right there," she said.

"I don't care who's standing there," he said. "I love you and I want everyone to know it."

Just then Carol and Charlotte came out of the kitchen to see what all of the excitement was about.

"Well, everyone knows it, now," Cat said.

"Ask me some more questions," Jim said.

"OK. What is your favorite food?" Cat asked.

"That's easy," Jim answered. "You. You're my food when I'm hungry and my drink when I'm thirsty. I only live because of you, my Darling," Jim said, as he looked into Cat's eyes. "If you were to ever leave me, then I would die."

Everyone had been laughing at Jim until he had gotten so

serious, but the laughter immediately stopped and the room was silent, as Jim took the package out of his pocket and handed it to Cat. "Happy anniversary, Darling. I know it's early, but I couldn't wait. I guess you thought I wouldn't remember, but I did."

Cat took the box and started to cry. "Oh, Jim, I was afraid you wouldn't remember."

"Don't just stand there crying," Jim said. "Open it. I want to see if you like it."

"Oh, Jim. I love it," she said, as she took the necklace from the box and held it up to see it better. "It's perfect. Here, put it on me."

"I'm glad you like it," he said quietly, as he fastened it around her neck. "Mark helped me pick it out."

She turned and glanced at Mark and he turned red, ducked his head and backed out of the room.

"What were you doing in the kitchen?" he asked, changing the subject.

"We were getting things ready for Thanksgiving," she answered. "You know it's Thursday, the 28th, don't you?"

"Yes, I know," Jim answered. "I actually remembered that, too. You can go back to what you were doing, then. Mark and I need to go to my office and discuss some things."

When they were in Jim's office with the door shut, Jim asked, "What did you say to them to make them reinstate me?"

"I just told them the truth," Mark answered.

"I haven't completely gotten my memory back, but I do remember some of what happened. You must have really embellished the truth," Jim said.

"Like I said, Jim. I told them the truth. That and your unblemished record did the trick. I didn't lie for you, Jim. I just told them what I saw."

"Mark, I need to know the whole story. I still don't remember much, but I know there's something you're not telling me," Jim said. "I think it has something to do with Cat, because every time I try to remember, I see her face. Tell me, Mark. I need to know."

"Jim, you don't need to know. You don't even want to know," Mark tried to talk him out of it.

"Mark, I mean it. I want to know. I have to know for my own peace of mind. What does Cat have to do with this?" Jim asked.

"OK, Jim. You win. You're not going to like it, though," Mark finally gave in.

"When Orretese had you tied up, he was beating you to a pulp. I was unconscious. They had already knocked me out. They kept trying to get you to give them the code, but you wouldn't talk. Then one of them got the bright idea of bringing Cat to make you talk," Mark continued.

"What do you mean bring Cat? Bring Cat where?" Jim asked.

"Bring her there to make you talk," Mark answered.

"What happened to Cat when he brought her there? I think I remember." Jim was trembling now.

When Mark didn't continue, Jim asked again, in a louder voice. "What did that scumbag do to Cat?"

"Do you want me to say it, Jim? I think you already know," Mark finished. Jim was barely breathing now as he asked, "Why didn't I kill him?"

"You almost did, Jim. That's why you were suspended," Mark said.

"I can't believe I didn't. If I had known what I was going to be going through, I would have. I would have finished the job I started. I would have beat him to death."

"No, Jim. I wouldn't have let you," Mark said. "I shouldn't have let you go as long as I did."

"You couldn't have stopped me, Mark. I would have killed you, too," Jim looked at Mark with hatred in his eyes.

"When is his trial? Have they set a date yet?" Jim asked.

"It's some time in February. I don't remember the exact date," Mark answered.

"I'm going to get well, Mark. I'm going to be completely well by then. I'm putting that guy away for a long time. He'll never see the outside of prison for the rest of his life," Jim said through clenched teeth. "I promise, Mark, if that's the last thing I do, and it may very well be."

CHAPTER 6

November 21 finally arrived. Since Carol and Cat had had a double wedding, Carol suggested that they celebrate their first-year anniversary together by going to a really fancy restaurant. Jim had begun to remember things that happened before his surgery and was on his way to recovery.

Since there were no really fancy restaurants in Brookville, they decided to make the long trip to Memphis. So Cat called and made reservations for the six of them for that night. It was a fancy restaurant, so the men wore tuxedos and the ladies wore formal gowns. Cat wore her heart-shaped anniversary necklace and Charlotte wore a diamond necklace, bracelet and earrings. Carol didn't go for a lot of jewelry, so she only wore a small pendant and her wedding rings.

On the way to Memphis, everyone talked and laughed and enjoyed themselves. Jim was finally getting back to his old self. He drove and Tyler rode in front with him, while Skip rode in back with the ladies. It was a tight fit, but since he was the smallest male, it only made sense that he would ride in back.

At the restaurant, Jim ordered a bottle of Champagne to toast their one-year anniversary. Everyone ordered a steak, baked potato and a green salad. They had heard that this restaurant was famous for its steaks.

Halfway through their meal, four masked gunmen, carrying AK-47 assault rifles, burst into the restaurant.

"Everyone stay where you are," one of them demanded. Another one locked the exit so no one was able to escape.

"You girls, get under the table," Jim said quickly, and Cat, Carol and Charlotte quickly obeyed. Then he, Tyler and Skip stood up in front of the table to block the gunmen's view of the women.

"Charlotte, help me get my necklace off," Cat said. "I can't let them take it or my rings. I'll hide them in my shoe," Cat said.

"OK, but I have too much to hide in my shoe. What can I do?" Charlotte asked, as she unclasped Cat's necklace.

"I don't know, Charlotte," Cat answered, as she put her necklace and rings in her shoe.

"Do something, Jim," Tyler urged. "Do you have your weapon?"

"Be quiet, Tyler," Jim said. "There are too many of them and too many people to get hurt."

"Skip and I'll help you," Tyler persisted. "Do something. Charlotte has a bunch of jewelry on and I have $2,000 in my wallet."

"Just shut up, Tyler," Jim said, as he tried to quiet Tyler. "The police will be here soon. They've been alerted."

Soon the robbers made their way around the room and got to where Jim, Tyler and Skip were standing. "Where's your women?" the robber said in a gruff voice. "I know you didn't come here dressed like that with no date. Where are they?"

Jim just stood there without saying a word, but Tyler gave him a slight nudge.

"Move out away from the table," the robber demanded, as he urged them over with his weapon.

Now, he could see the women huddled under the table. "Well, hello ladies," he said. "Come out and join the party. Hurry up and get out here."

As Cat, Charlotte and Carol emerged from under the table, the gunman recognized Charlotte.

"Hey, what have we got here," he said. "We've got us a genuine movie star. Hey, guys, it's Charlotte Reynolds, the movie star, in person."

"Don't touch her," Tyler said, as he lunged toward the gunman.

"Well now, I guess she must belong to you," the gunman said, as he hit Tyler with his weapon and knocked him down. "Yeah, I think I seen you in that movie, too. Didn't I?"

"Hey, guys, we've hit the jackpot," the gunman said.

"You don't know who you're dealing with," Tyler said, as he picked himself up off the floor.

Jim tried to get him to be quiet, but he continued. "He's a Federal Agent. He'll make you sorry you did that. Do something, Jim."

"A Federal Agent, huh?" the gunman asked. "Well, let's just see if you're carrying a weapon."

Now, Jim had no other alternative than to try to subdue the gunman. He wrestled with him and there was a shot and the gunman fell to the floor. The ladies screamed and blood oozed from the gunman's wound.

"Hey, D," one of the other gunmen called. "You all right?"

When D didn't answer, the other gunman called to the others, "Let's get out of here. No one was supposed to get killed."

As they ran toward the exit, the police stormed into the restaurant with their guns drawn. They placed the remaining robbers in handcuffs and retrieved the stolen money and jewelry.

"Tyler, if you ever do that again, I'll beat you within an inch of your life," Jim said through clenched teeth.

"Well, I saved Charlotte's jewelry and our money, didn't I?" Tyler said in his defense.

"I told you the police would be here soon. There was no need for anyone to be killed," Jim said angrily.

"How did you know that they would be here for sure?" Tyler asked.

"Because I alerted them," Jim answered.

One of the police officers approached Jim and asked, "Commander Ryan, is this yours?" he said pointing to the dead robber.

"Yes, I'm sorry to say," Jim answered and then he and the officer walked out of earshot and discussed the shooting.

When Jim returned, he said, "I gave them all the information they needed from us, for now. Come on, let's get out of here. They don't need us anymore." Then he urged them toward the exit before the news media arrived.

On the drive home, Tyler sat in back with the women and Skip rode up front with Jim. Tyler was still peeved at Jim and didn't want to say anything to him.

Cat was thankful that Jim was finally coming back to the old Jim she knew and loved. He was finally taking command again. She had hopes now that he would soon be well.

That night Jim made love to her more passionately than he had since they had returned from their honeymoon.

On Monday morning, Detective Bryan Adams, of the Memphis Police Department called and asked Jim if he and the others could come to the police station. They needed to ask them some questions about the shooting incident.

When they arrived at police headquarters, Detective Adams asked Jim to give his version of the shooting first.

"Well," Jim began. "It was our first-year anniversary and I had taken them to the restaurant to celebrate. We were about halfway through our meal when these four gunmen, wearing masks and carrying AK-47 assault rifles, entered the restaurant and told us all to stay where we were and that it was a robbery.

"I told the girls to hide under the table and Tyler, Skip and I stood in front of them to hide them. When one of the gunmen made his way around to us, he wanted to know where our women were. When we didn't answer, he forced us to move and spotted the girls. He made them come out and, the one I shot, recognized Charlotte and made a big deal about a movie star being there.

"Tyler told the guy that I was a Federal Agent and to leave his wife alone. The guy told me to give him my weapon. I refused. We fought over the gun and it discharged, killing the assailant."

"So what you're saying, is that it was an accident that the suspect was shot? Am I correct in saying that?" Detective Adams asked.

"That's correct," Jim answered.

"That'll be all for you. Now, let's see if the others corroborate your story," Detective Adams said.

The next one to be questioned was Tyler. He wasn't very enthusiastic about the matter, but he knew he couldn't refuse.

"Now, Mr. Weldon, will you give me your version of the shooting incident?" Detective Adams began.

"OK," Tyler answered. "We were all celebrating their first anniversary. We were enjoying a good meal, when these goons crashed into the restaurant with masks on and heavily armed. They told everyone to stay where they were and put their valuables into a sack they had.

"When they came to us, they asked where our women were. They were under the table because Jim told them to hide there. When no one told them where they were, they made us move and saw the girls under the table.

"They made them come out, and when they saw Charlotte, they recognized her and the guy started shouting about having a movie star there. He started pawing my wife and I told him to leave her alone. He knocked me down and I tried to get Jim to do something, but I think he was afraid. He said there were too many of them and too many people.

"Then the guy saw Jim's gun and tried to take it. Jim fought him, the gun went off and the guy was dead."

"Then you feel like it was an accident?" Detective Adams asked.

"Of course it was an accident," Tyler said. "You don't think Jim would kill the guy in front of us, on purpose, do you?"

"No, I guess he wouldn't," Detective Adams answered. "That's all I need from you. Would you please send Mr. Taylor in? I want to question him next."

"It's your turn, Skip," Tyler said when he came back into the room where they were all waiting.

When Skip entered the interrogation room, Detective Adams said, "Mr. Taylor, don't be nervous. I just want to get your version of the shooting incident. Just tell me in your own words what happened."

"All I know is that we were enjoying our anniversary meal and these thugs burst into the restaurant and ruined it," Skip began. "Carol, my wife, and I had a double wedding with Cat and Jim. It was our first-year anniversary. We were all having a good time when, like I said, these goons burst into the restaurant and ruined it."

"Can you tell me more about the shooting?" Detective Adams asked.

"When Jim saw the guns the guys had, he told the girls to hide under the table. When it was our turn to give them our valuables, they wanted to know where the girls were. We didn't tell them, so they shoved us out of the way and found them.

"The guy made a big deal about Charlotte and Tyler being movie stars. I was behind Tyler and Jim and I don't know what started it, but Jim and the guy fought over Jim's gun. I heard it go off and the goon fell on the floor. Jim checked his pulse and said he was dead. The others got scared and ran. The police were coming in at the same time and caught them. Well, you know the rest because you were there."

"Do you feel that Mr. Ryan shot the suspect by accident?" Detective Adams asked.

"As far as I could tell, Jim was trying to keep the suspect, as you call him, from killing him and us. I guess it was an accident that the guy got shot, but if he hadn't, he probably would have shot Jim. I would say it was self-defense."

"Thank you, Mr. Taylor. That's all I need from you," Detective Adams said. "Will you please send in Mrs. Ryan?"

"Mrs. Ryan," Detective Adams began when Cat entered the interrogation room and sat down. "Don't be nervous. I'm just going to ask you a few questions and I want you to answer them as truthfully as you can. Do you understand?"

When Cat said yes, she understood, Detective Adams continued. "I just want you to give me your version of the shooting incident involving your husband, Commander Jim Ryan, and the suspect."

"Well," she began. "Carol, my younger sister, and I had a double wedding and Jim had taken us to that restaurant to celebrate our one-year anniversary. We were enjoying our meal, when all of a sudden, these four men came in wearing masks and carrying big guns. I don't know what you call them. Anyway, they came into the restaurant and told us all to stay where we were; they were going to rob us.

"Jim was afraid they might do something to us girls, because we were wearing jewelry, so he told us to hide under the table. I had on my beautiful necklace that Jim had just given me for our anniversary. I didn't want to lose it, so I took it and my rings off and hid them in my shoe. Charlotte had too much jewelry on to hide it, though.

"Anyway, when they got to us, the one guy, the one that Jim shot, he said, 'Where are your women? You didn't come here dressed like that without a date.' Jim didn't say anything, so he made him, Tyler and Skip move over so he could see under the table. He saw us under there and made us get out.

"When Charlotte, my older sister, came out, he recognized her from her movies. She's a movie star, you know. Anyway, he started yelling to the other robbers that he had a movie star there.

"I don't know how he knew that Jim had a gun, but somehow he saw it and ordered him to give it to him. Jim refused and he tried to take it away from Jim. Somehow, the gun went off and the robber got shot. Is that all you want to know?" Cat asked.

"Yes, thank you, Mrs. Ryan," Detective Adams said. "You may go now. Would you please send in Ms. Reynolds?"

Cat returned to the waiting area and told Charlotte it was her turn.

"How was it?" Charlotte asked. "What did they ask you?"

"You'll find out. Just go on in, Charlotte. It wasn't difficult," Cat answered.

As Charlotte entered the interrogation room, Detective Adams indicated a chair and asked her to be seated.

"Now, Ms. Reynolds, or do you prefer Mrs. Weldon?" Detective Adams asked."

"Either is correct," she answered.

"OK, Ms. Reynolds, I want you to tell me about the shooting incident in your own words," Detective Adams said.

"Where do you want me to begin?" Charlotte asked.

"At the beginning," Detective Adams said.

"OK. We were celebrating Cat's and Carol's one-year wedding anniversary. They had had a double wedding. That's why they had the same anniversary. Jim, Cat's husband, had taken us to this restaurant. He said that they were famous for their steaks, and we all love steak.

"Anyway, we had just begun to enjoy our meal, when these terrible men with masks on and carrying big guns came storming into the restaurant and told us all to stay where we were. It was horrible. It was the most awful experience I have ever had in my life. I thought I would pass out.

"Then the men started on the other side of the room making the women give them their jewelry and the men give them their wallets. Jim didn't want anything to happen to us, so he told us to get under the table. He doesn't like for anyone to touch Cat. He gets really angry when anyone touches her. Well, not just anyone. You know what I mean. When a man touches her.

"Well, anyway, we got under the table like Jim told us to do.

"Cat took the necklace that Jim had just given to her off and put it into her shoe. I had a lot of jewelry on and didn't have room in my shoe for it, so I just left it on.

"When one of the robbers got to our table, he asked 'Where are your women? I know you didn't come here without a date.' No one answered and so he pushed them away from the table and saw us all huddled there. I think that's when Jim got really mad.

"When I crawled out, the guy recognized me and started yelling to the other guys that he found a movie star. Tyler, my husband told them to leave me alone and the guy knocked Tyler down to the floor. I guess that was when Jim pulled out his gun. I really don't know because the guy was making such a fuss about my being a movie star.

"Anyway, the guy saw Jim's gun and turned me loose and grabbed at Jim's gun. There was a terrible fight and the gun went off. I screamed and the guy fell down with blood all over him and the floor.

"The other robbers ran when they saw he had been shot. That's when you and the police officers broke in and arrested the other ones."

"Do you think Commander Ryan shot the suspect by accident, then?" Detective Adams asked.

"Well, of course he did," Charlotte answered. "Do you think he would deliberately shoot him right in front of us?"

"You said that he was angry when the suspect touched his wife, didn't you?" Detective Adams asked.

"Yes, of course he was angry," Charlotte said. "Wouldn't you be if that guy was trying to rough up your wife? Tyler sure got mad when he put his hands on me."

"You still feel like the shooting was accidental, though? Even if Commander Ryan was angry?" Detective Adams persisted.

"Yes, I'm sure it was," Charlotte answered. She was afraid, now that she might have said something that she shouldn't have said. She hoped that she hadn't gotten Jim into trouble by saying that he was angry when he shot the robber.

"You may leave now, Ms. Reynolds. Will you please send in Mrs. Taylor?" Detective Adams asked.

"Carol, it's your turn," Charlotte said, as she returned to the waiting area.

"Come on in and sit down, Mrs. Taylor," Detective Adams said when Carol entered.

"Now, there's nothing to be afraid about. I'm not going to bite you.

I just want to ask you a few questions about the shooting incident," Detective Adams said. "Do you remember what happened?"

"Yes, I remember," Carol answered.

"Will you tell me, in your own words, what happened?"

"Yes, of course," Carol said. "My sister, Cat, and I were celebrating our one-year anniversary with our husbands and sister, Charlotte, and her husband. Jim had made a reservation for us and he had also driven us there.

"We were eating our dinner and laughing and having a good time, when these four masked men burst into the restaurant carrying big guns. I think Skip said they were AK-47 assault rifles, or something like that. I don't really know one from the other.

"They started across the room from us and told everyone to put their jewelry and money in a sack that they had.

"Jim told Cat, Charlotte and me to hide under the table. We did and Cat took off her jewelry and put it in her shoe, but Charlotte said she had too much on to try to hide it.

"When that guy came over to where the men were standing, he asked them where their dates were. When they didn't answer him, he pushed them out of the way and saw us under the table. The guy made us come out and when he saw Charlotte, he got real excited. He yelled at the others to come see. He said he had found a movie star.

"I was behind Cat and Charlotte, so I didn't see what happened next. All I know is that somehow Jim and the robber started fighting over Jim's gun. Then, all of a sudden, it went off and the robber was lying on the floor with blood all over him.

"Jim felt of his pulse and said he was dead. The others saw the guy get shot and ran, but you and the other police officers caught them and you know the rest."

"You said that you didn't see what started the confrontation. Is that correct?" Detective Adams asked.

"Yes, that's what I said," Carol answered. "I don't know how the robber knew that Jim had a gun and I don't know if Jim pulled it on him or what. I just know they were fighting over it and it went off."

"Thank you, Mrs. Taylor. That will be all. You may return to the waiting area. Will you please tell Commander Ryan that I would like to see him now?" Detective Adams said.

"Commander Ryan, your witnesses have corroborated your story. The shooting of the robbery suspect will be ruled as an accidental shooting," Detective Adams said. "There is one thing I would like to ask you about, though. One of your witnesses mentioned that you were angry before the shooting. Did this have any bearing on the outcome of your struggle with the suspect?"

"No, of course not," Jim answered. "I was angry because Tyler was pushing me to do something. When my weapon discharged, it was because the suspect had his finger on the trigger. Not because I was trying to shoot him. I did not shoot the guy on purpose. I want you to believe me. My career depends on what you believe about that shooting. Do you believe me?"

"Yes, Commander Ryan, I do believe you," Detective Adams answered. "I just wanted to make sure. You and your family may go now. I'll contact you, if I need any further information."

When Jim returned to the waiting area, he said, "Let's go." Then he headed toward the exit. Cat could tell he was angry about something, but she knew he wouldn't say anything.

After they were in the car and headed home, Cat hazarded a meek, "How did it go, Jim?"

"I'll talk to you later," he said. That was all she got out of him.

When they arrived home, Jim was still angry. He dropped Carol, Skip, Charlotte and Tyler off at their cabin and then took Cat back to their cabin.

When he walked into the cabin, Cat prepared for the storm she knew was coming.

Jim paced up and down in the den before saying anything. Then he exploded. "Tyler almost cost me my job, Cat," he said angrily.

"How did Tyler do that?" she asked trying to calm him down.

"He tried to get me to show my hand back at the restaurant. He wanted me to try to arrest those gunmen single-handedly. Someone told that detective that I was angry when I shot the guy. He thought I did it on purpose. It was an accident, Cat. We were fighting to gain control of my weapon and it discharged. It was an accident."

"I know that, Jim," Cat said. "You don't have to convince me."

"I'm so mad at Tyler, I could beat him to a pulp," Jim said.

"What did Detective Adams say he was going to do?" Cat asked.

"He said he was going to report it as an accident." Jim was cooling off a little now. "He didn't really believe me, though. I think he believes I shot the guy on purpose, but he said my witnesses corroborated my story, so he has to report it as an accident," Jim answered.

"Well, you're OK, then," Cat said.

"Not really," Jim said. "As long as he believes I did it on purpose, he may try to prove that I did. I could be in a lot of trouble, Cat. All because of that creep, Tyler."

Somehow the news media got a tip that Charlotte and Tyler had been in the restaurant when the robbery occurred. It was in the newspapers and on TV. Reporters found out where they were staying and hounded them for an interview. At first, they were pleased, because they thought it would be good publicity for their new movie, but after several days of it, they were tired of it and decided to return to Hollywood. Jim was almost back to his old self again and Christmas was getting close. Since Charlotte and Tyler had celebrated Thanksgiving with Charlotte's family, Tyler wanted to celebrate Christmas with his family, who lived in California. Jim was more than happy to see them go. He and Tyler had tangled again and Jim swore that if he didn't leave soon, he would kill him. So, the week before Christmas, Jim and Cat drove Charlotte and Tyler to the airport to catch their flight back to Hollywood.

Skip also said that he would like to spend Christmas with his family, so he and Carol left for Plainview the same day.

Mark didn't have anywhere to go, so he asked if he could spend

Christmas with Jim and Cat. They said of course, but they weren't going to do anything special, since everyone else was leaving.

Barbara and Molly wanted to spend some time with their families, so Cat told them to go, also. She said that she could prepare the meals for no more than there would be for Christmas, so, for the first time since Cat and Jim had returned from their honeymoon, it would be just the two of them and Mark.

Cat fixed a wonderful meal of roast turkey, cornbread dressing and all the trimmings. After the meal, they sat in the den and exchanged gifts. Cat had gotten a warm sweater made of soft cashmere for Jim and a pair of warm gloves for Mark.

As they were sitting in the den watching a football game on TV, there was a knock at the door. When Cat answered it, there stood Jenny Long shivering in the cold wind. "Hi, Jenny," Cat said. "Hurry up and get in here out of the cold. I never expected to see you today."

"Well, I've been on another assignment and have been out of state," she answered.

When Cat returned to the den with Jenny following her, Jim said, "Hi, Jenny." Mark got to his feet and walked over to Jenny and gave her a quick kiss. "Hi, Jenny," he said. "Come sit down." Then he led her to a spot where he had been sitting.

"You two seem pretty friendly," Jim commented.

"We've been dating for a while," Mark answered.

"Oh, you have, have you?" Jim asked. "How long has this been going on?"

"About a month now," Mark answered.

"I see," Jim said. Then he changed the subject.

After Jenny visited with Jim and Cat for a while, Mark said, "Come on, Jenny. Let's see what's happening downtown." Then he took her hand and helped her to her feet.

As they headed toward the door, Mark turned around and said, "Don't wait up for me. I have a key, I can let myself in." Then he and Jenny were gone.

"Well, I guess Mark and Jenny are an item, now," Cat said. "I'm surprised that they have been dating for a month and we didn't know it."

"We've been busy with our own lives, Cat," Jim said. "We didn't have time to bother about what was going on in Mark's life. I'm glad he found someone as nice as Jenny."

"Yes, I am, too," Cat said. "He's really a nice guy."

"Yeah, the nicest," Jim said, then he changed the subject again.

When they went upstairs to bed, Cat took her unopened Christmas gift from Jim with her. He had suggested that she wait until they were alone before she opened it. When she opened it, she saw a beautiful, sheer red teddy. "Thank you for suggesting that I wait until we were alone to open it. I would have been embarrassed to have opened it in front of Mark," Cat said, as she kissed and thanked him for the gift.

"Go put it on," he said and he lay back on the bed and waited for her. When she came out of the bathroom with it on, he caught his breath and said, "You look just like I thought you would in it. You look gorgeous. Come here." Then he pulled her down and kissed her passionately and urgently. Soon she was lost in his love.

Afterward, he turned over and went to sleep, and Cat went into the bathroom and took a long, hot bath. When she got into bed, she lay there awake for a long time thinking about Jim and how much he had changed since his illness. She was glad that he was finally on his way back to becoming the Jim with whom she had fallen in love. She knew that he would soon be back to the work schedule that he had had before, also. She had mixed feelings about that. She knew he had a job to do, but she hated that it was such a dangerous job.

She was still awake about 3:00 a.m. when she heard one of the steps on the staircase creak. She heard someone trying to walk softly up the stairs and down the hall, but he wasn't doing a very good job of it.

"Well, I guess Mark and Jenny had a good time," she thought. "They sure made a night of it."

Then she went to sleep. She felt like a mother who had waited for her son to return home from a date. Now that he was safe back at home, she could relax and go to sleep. The next thing she knew, it was morning.

CHAPTER 7

On Monday morning, Mark headed to Jim's office and asked if Jim was going to accompany him.

"Yeah, I need to start getting back into the harness," Jim answered.

When they had entered the office and shut the door, Mark asked Jim when he wanted to take over his commander duties again.

"I have to see Dr. Johnson after the first of the year and get his approval. Then I have to appear before the Review Board again and get their approval. I hope it'll be soon. I'm getting bored having nothing to do."

"Well, I'll gladly give the reins back to you when you're ready," Mark said.

Then Jim changed the subject. "You and Jenny seemed pretty close at Christmas. You got something going with her?"

"Well, it's like they say, 'If you can't be with the one you love, love the one you're with,' Mark said and gave Jim a wry smile.

Jim didn't say anything, but he gave Mark a look that meant he didn't like Mark's comment. Then he let it drop and changed the subject again.

"What do you have for today?" Jim asked.

"We've been watching a couple of dissidents who are in an apartment on Beach Street," Mark answered, as he logged into the computer and pulled up the screen he wanted.

"They've been purchasing bomb-making material. It looks as

though they're about ready to do something. I have a raid set up for tonight. I thought we'd let Cat go. Just to give her some experience."

"No, Cat can't go," Jim said adamantly.

"Why not, Jim?" Mark asked. "She can shoot as well as anyone else on the team. She's even better than some."

"Shooting at a target is different from shooting at a person who can shoot back at you," Jim answered.

"She either needs to start going out with us, or you're going to have to let her go," Mark answered.

"Did someone tell you that?" Jim asked.

"Director Halbert told me," Mark answered.

"Well, she isn't ready yet," Jim said. "This is my unit and I do what's best for each of my team members. I say she isn't ready yet and she doesn't go yet," Jim said, getting angry.

"Suit yourself, Jim," Mark answered. "You're the boss. I'm just telling you what the Director said."

"All right, if I let her go, will you and the guys watch her and make sure nothing happens to her?" Jim finally gave in.

"Yes, of course, you know we will, Jim," Mark said. "I'll watch her as closely as you would. I care for her, too, you know," Mark said without thinking. Then he apologized, "I'm sorry, Jim. I shouldn't have said that that way. You know what I mean, though."

"Yeah, I know what you mean," Jim sighed. "It's OK for you to care for her, just don't ever do anything about it."

"You know I'm loyal to you, Jim," Mark said. "I would never deliberately do anything to hurt you. If you want me to transfer to another unit, I will. If, knowing how I feel about Cat as I do, prevents you from continuing to work with me, just say the word and I'll be gone. Forget I said what I did."

"No, I don't want you to transfer. Just remember that she's my wife," Jim said through clenched teeth.

"Then forget what I said. Just remember that I will watch out for her," Mark said.

Although Jim was angry with Mark, he let it drop. Mark had

been loyal to him for a long time. He had never seen him say or do anything to Cat that he thought was inappropriate. He was just so darn jealous of Cat. He had to stop it before it got any worse.

Jim knew Mark was right about letting Cat go with them. He just trembled at the thought of putting her in danger again. Maybe he should never have let her join his unit. Maybe he should always make her stay at home with someone there to protect her. He would have to remember not to let Mark stay there with her anymore, though. He didn't like the idea of Mark ever being alone with her, now that he knew how Mark felt about her. Of course, he couldn't blame him. It was easy to fall in love with Cat. He knew from experience.

"Cat, can you come here for a few minutes?" Jim called from the door of his office.

"Sure, Jim," Cat replied. "I'll be right there."

"Come on in and sit down," Jim said and motioned to a chair. "Do you think you're ready yet?" Jim asked.

"Ready for what?" Cat asked.

"Ready to go on an assignment with my team? Mark thinks you're ready," Jim said.

"Yes, oh yes, Jim," she enthused. "Yes, I would love to go on a mission with you. You are going, too, aren't you?"

"Yes, I'll be going, too," Jim replied. "I need to get back into the harness before I take command again."

"Thank you, Mark, for the vote of confidence," Cat said. "I'll try to live up to your expectations."

"OK, Cat," Jim said, as he led her out of his office. "Let's go to headquarters and get you outfitted. Mark, you stay here and finish getting things together."

"Sure, Jim," Mark said, a little peeved at Jim because he had already finished making the plan. All he needed to do now was get the team together, which would have taken only a few minutes. He would have liked to have gone with Jim and Cat, but he figured Jim was still angry with him. Anyway, he hoped that Cat didn't prove him wrong. Jim would never let him forget it, if she did.

At headquarters, Jim took Cat around and introduced her to everyone. Then he took her to where the gear was stored and picked out a bulletproof vest, a weapon and other gear that she would need.

"Now, Cat, you'll only be an observer tonight," Jim told her when they had returned back home.

"Yeah, Cat," Mark said. "You'll remain in the vehicle with Jim and observe. Jim hasn't been officially approved to return to work yet. Isn't that right, Jim?"

"Yes, that's right, Cat," Jim said, as he gave Mark a dirty look. Mark was letting Jim know that he was still in charge, even if Jim would be accompanying the team on this assignment.

When the team arrived at the suspects' apartment, Jim and Cat remained in the vehicle while Mark and the others surrounded the building. Jim kept up a running description of what was happening for Cat. He knew the procedure all too well, because he had led the team in the same procedure many times before. He was itching to be out with them, but he knew he could be dismissed unless he waited until after he was approved to go back to work by the Review Board.

The mission went smoothly, until one of the suspects got away. Jim wanted to go after him, but he saw Mark in pursuit. Jim and Cat watched as Mark handled the situation in exactly the same manner that Jim would have handled it. Jim was proud of Mark, even though he was a little jealous. He could hardly wait until he was back in command again.

CHAPTER 8

Cat, Jim and Mark spent New Year's Day watching football on TV. Jenny came by and she and Mark left for a while. They returned around 6:00 p.m. and Cat fixed hamburgers and French fries for everyone.

After she ate and visited again for a while, Jenny said she had to go. She had an early assignment in the morning. Mark walked her to her car and then returned to the den where Cat and Jim were still watching football.

"Jim, I need to get ready for tomorrow," Mark said, as he headed toward Jim's office.

"I'll come with you," Jim said, as he followed him into the office and shut the door.

"What have you got for tomorrow?" Jim asked.

"We need to rescue someone from North Korea," Mark said matter-of-factly.

"North Korea?" Jim asked. "Can't it wait until I'm back in command?"

"No, Jim," answered Mark. "It can't wait."

"I go see Dr. Johnson next week and then I go before the Board," Jim replied. "I don't see why it can't wait until I'm approved to command again."

"Jim, when you made me Acting Commander, you agreed to let me make my own decisions, did you not?" Mark asked.

"Yes, but I expected you to make good decisions," Jim said,

beginning to get angry. "This isn't a good decision. Have you ever tried to get in and out of North Korea? It's almost impossible and very dangerous. You need to wait until I'm ready to command."

Mark was silent for a few minutes and then he said, "Jim, you were my teacher and you were a darn good one. You need to trust me on this and believe that I have learned what you have taught me. I can do it, Jim. Now, let me do my job and you go be with your wife while you have the chance. Besides, the Director ordered me and our unit to go. We leave for the base the first thing in the morning. From there, we board a C17 for our trip to Seoul, South Korea. We stop in Seattle to refuel and get ready for the long trip to Seoul. When we arrive at Osan Air Base, we'll take a day to plan our rescue operations. When we have a plan, then we'll go. Don't worry. Everything will work out just fine."

Now, Jim was very angry. He knew that Mark was making a mistake, but he had to pay for his own mistakes. Jim remembered the mistakes he had made when he first became Commander. He regretted some of them still, but Mark had to make his own mistakes, so Jim walked out of the office and slammed the door. As much as he hated it, he would have to let Mark make his own mistakes.

The next week was Jim's appointment with Dr. Johnson. He could tell that he was getting better, therefore he was certain that the doctor would release him to go back to work. He was ready and anxious to go back to work. He was a workaholic and these days when he wasn't working were harder on him than his injury was.

Dr. Johnson tested his memory by asking him to repeat some random words. He had him walk across the room to see how straight he could walk. He checked his wound and said that it was healing nicely.

After carefully examining him, Dr. Johnson declared Jim well enough to resume his duties as Commander of his unit. He gave him a written approval, which was required before the Board would approve his return to active duty.

When Jim and Cat left Dr. Johnson's office, Jim was walking

on air. He grabbed Cat and swung her around. "I can go back to work now, Cat," he said happily. You won't have to put up with my grumpy old face any longer. Well, if the Board approves, that is. I'm sure they will approve, too."

Jim made an appointment with the Board and he and Cat arrived for his appointment the next day. Cat remained in the waiting area, while Jim nervously went into the Boardroom.

Jim gave the Commissioner the letter of approval from Dr. Johnson and he read it and passed it to the other members. Then they asked Jim some questions about his health. They wanted to know if he felt that he was able to carry out his assigned duties, to which Jim answered a resounding, "Yes, Sir."

After the preliminaries, they got down to the serious matters.

"Commander Ryan, we have been notified about a shooting incident you were involved in during your recuperation. It happened in a restaurant. Can you give us your version of the incident?"

"Yes, Sir, I can," Jim replied.

"I was dining with my family and these four masked gunmen entered the restaurant and announced that they were going to rob us all. When they got to me and my family, they discovered that I was a Federal Agent and found my weapon. We fought over my weapon and it accidentally discharged. The gunman was hit and didn't survive his wound. Is that all, you need to know, Sir?"

"So, you say it was an accident that the gun was discharged?" the Commissioner asked.

"Yes, Sir. It was," Jim replied.

"You weren't angry that you and your family were being robbed?" the Commissioner asked.

"Yes, Sir, I was angry. Wouldn't you have been angry?" Jim answered. "I did not kill the guy on purpose, though. I would never have deliberately killed someone in front of my family."

"No, I guess you wouldn't. Will you step out into the waiting area for a few minutes, while we make our decision?" the Commissioner asked, as he led Jim to the door.

After about an hour, the Commissioner called Jim back into the Boardroom.

"Upon careful deliberation, the Board has decided to approve you, Commander James Ryan, to return to your full duties, starting tomorrow. You will retain your Commander title and the same salary you were getting before your injury," the Commissioner said. "Do you have any questions?"

"No, Sir," Jim said. "I'm just happy to be working again. I thank each one of you for putting your trust in me and I will try, to the best of my ability, to fulfill my position adequately, as I have in the past."

"We do recommend that you make an appointment with the staff psychiatrist again. We feel that you still have some issues that you need to resolve. We will leave it to you to decide whether to take our recommendation or not," the Commissioner said.

"Thank you again, Sir," Jim answered. "I will consider your recommendation."

Then he walked out to where Cat was waiting for him. He could hardly contain his happiness. He hugged and kissed her and said, "I'm back in, Cat. Let's go home."

When they arrived back at the cabin, Ted called.

"Jim, I'm sure glad you're back," Ted said.

"What's wrong, Ted?" Jim asked.

"It's Mark. He's been taken prisoner," Ted answered.

"What happened?" Jim asked, as he went into his office and shut the door. Cat wanted to follow, but she knew that Jim wouldn't let her, so she went into the den and waited.

Ted began as soon as Jim sat down at his computer and brought up the layout of North Korea. "When we arrived at Osan AB in South Korea, we were briefed on the plan to rescue the kidnapped diplomat, who had been taken as a prisoner to North Korea. We were to fly in a Huey helicopter northeast from Seoul along the coastline of the Sea of Japan, then north, crossing secretly into North Korea near the city of Wonsan, North Korea. It was determined that the diplomat was being held in a compound there.

"We did as instructed and found the place where they were holding the hostage," Ted continued. "We waited till dark and surrounded the place where they were holding him. They must have been tipped off that we were coming, because they were ready for us. They had a trap set for us. As soon as we got close to the guy, they surrounded us.

"There was a fierce gun battle. Some of our team members were hit. Mark told us to get the diplomat and get out. Mark stayed behind to cover us. The last I saw of him, they had captured him and were beating him. We made it out with the diplomat, but Mark didn't make it to the chopper. They were firing at us as we were taking off. The chopper sustained some damage."

"Where are the others now?" Jim asked.

"They're at Osan AB waiting for you. Some of the guys were wounded, but they want to go back and get Mark," Ted answered. "I talked to the Director and asked him if you were cleared to return to active duty yet. He said that the Board had just cleared you to go back to work and that he would call you and give you orders to go to South Korea to lead the operation to rescue Mark."

"OK," Jim said. "Let me look at the area on the computer and see how things look. Then I'll grab my gear and get to Little Rock AFB as soon as I can. I should be at the base in about two hours. I'll see if I can schedule a C17 to take me to South Korea. I should be there by tomorrow. Can you and the unit be ready to go as soon as I get there?"

"Yes, Sir. We're ready to go now. We were just waiting for you," Ted answered.

"Here's the compound," Jim said, as he spotted an image that had to be the compound on the computer screen. "Where's Mark?"

"The last time I saw him, he was in that large building in the middle of the compound. Do you see the one I mean?" Ted asked, as he waited for Jim to locate the building he meant.

"Is there anything else you need?" Jim asked as he scanned his computer.

"No, Sir. We're just waiting for you," Ted answered.

As he ended the call with Ted, his phone rang again. Director Halbert asked him if he had talked to Ted yet. When Jim said that he had just talked to Ted, the director gave Jim his orders to fly to South Korea to rescue Mark.

Jim ended the call and hurried out of his office to gather his gear and tell Cat goodbye. When he opened the door of his office, Cat jumped up and hurried to him. "Where's Mark?" she asked.

"He's been captured," Jim answered. "Director Halbert has just given me orders to fly to South Korea and lead my team in the rescue operation in North Korea."

"Let me go, too, Jim," Cat pleaded. "I can help."

"No, Cat, it's too dangerous," Jim said, as he hurried toward the cabin door.

"Jim, let me go. Please let me go," Cat pleaded again.

"Cat, I don't have time to argue with you. You can't go and that's final. I made that mistake with your father. I'm not going to make the same mistake with you," Jim said, as he continued to gather his gear and head toward the door.

"I'm not my father," Cat yelled to Jim's back, but Jim just turned, kissed Cat and continued on out the door. He threw his gear into the trunk of his vehicle, jumped into the driver's seat and slammed the door. Before Cat could say anything else, Jim started the engine and tore out of the driveway, scattering gravel everywhere.

As Jim drove off, Cat started to cry. "Why couldn't he let me go help?" she said, remembering how her father had almost been captured when Jim had sent him on a secret mission to Russia and how badly it had turned out. As she kicked a rock in the driveway, she said, "I'm not my father. I could've helped."

When Jim arrived at Little Rock AFB, a C17 took him on the long journey to South Korea. At the Osan AB, Jim called the whole team together to show them the plan for rescuing Mark.

Some of his team were wounded so badly that they would be

unable to accompany them on the mission. After eliminating the wounded, Jim found that he had six able-bodied men.

"OK, men," Jim said. "You've been there before, so you know what it's like. Is there anyone who doesn't want to go on this mission?"

The men all said a resounding, "No, Sir," in unison.

"OK, let's go," Jim said encouragingly.

They all loaded into the chopper and were off. "They'll be expecting us again," Jim told his team. "We'll have to go in as quietly as we can. I'm sure Mark will be well guarded. When we get there, Ted, you take Harris, Faulkner and Ward with you. I'll take the rest with me. We'll go in two different directions. At midnight, we'll converge on the building where Mark is." Everyone was silent after that. They all were deep in their private thoughts. They knew that some of them may not make it back out alive, but they had to try to rescue Mark, even if it did cost them their lives.

Jim had picked out a remote spot for their drop zone. He knew that they would have to walk for a mile to get to the compound, but he couldn't risk getting any closer.

Just before they reached the drop zone, Jim told them to get ready. "Try to get as close to your leader as possible," Jim said. "We don't want to be all strung out. We need to be as small a target as possible."

By the time they had made the hike to the compound, it was getting close to midnight. Jim took his men and went east and Ted went west with his men. Slowly, they converged on the building where Mark was being held. There was a window in the room where Mark was being held. Jim looked through it and saw that Mark was chained to the wall and there were two guards watching him, They each had an AK-47 assault rifle.

"That presents a problem," Jim said to his men. "We have to get the guards away from Mark somehow."

Wayne Bryant said, "I'll draw them away and you can get him while they're chasing me."

"No, Wayne. I can't let you do that. You would be like a sitting duck. I'll think of something else."

Then Jim decided to work his way in as quietly as he could and catch them off guard. "You men stay put until you hear gunfire and then come in as fast as you can. I'll try to hold them down while you break the chains and release Mark."

Then Jim inched his way slowly into the room behind the guards. One of them saw Jim and prepared to fire his weapon, but Jim shot first, then turned and fired at the other guard. His men rushed into the room and freed Mark. Mark was wounded and barely able to walk, but one man on each side of him helped him and they hurried out before the other guards arrived.

They hurried out to the rendezvous point and met the chopper just as it was landing. They hurriedly boarded and it took off with the guards in hot pursuit. In firing their weapons, the North Koreans hit the chopper several times, but it managed to get high enough before it was damaged too severely.

Several of the men sustained wounds, but their wounds weren't too serious. Back at the base, everyone was examined and their wounds were dressed. Mark had the worse wounds. His would probably take longer to heal.

"Thanks, Jim," Mark said when he was safely on his way back home. "I hate that you had to do that. If I had listened to you, it wouldn't have happened."

"That's OK, Mark," Jim answered. "Now, you'll probably never do it again. I think you've learned your lesson. We all have to make mistakes before we learn what to do and what not to do."

"Wow," Mark thought. "I expected him to be a lot angrier. I figured he would really read me the riot act. I guess he's mellowed some since his injury. Maybe now he'll show more mercy to the injured. Anyway, I'm glad he isn't riding me like I thought he would." Mark had a lot to think about on the long trip back home.

When they arrived at the cabin, Cat saw the vehicles pull into the yard and ran and opened the door. Ted and Bill carried Mark into the cabin and lay him on the sofa in the den.

"Mark, you're hurt," Cat said, as she hurried over to him. "Can I get you something? Do you want a pillow or an ice pack or heating pad or something?"

"Yeah," Mark replied, as he placed Cat's hand on his forehead. "I need some TLC."

Jim frowned and headed toward his office. "Come on Ted, let's get that report done," he said, as Ted followed him into the office.

"Don't let it bother you, Jim," Ted said. "I don't think he means anything by it."

"I know, Ted," Jim replied. "I still don't like it. She didn't even say hi to me or even ask if I was all right."

"You didn't give her a chance, Jim," Ted persisted. "Just forget it, OK?"

Then Cat knocked on the door and said, "Jim, are you all right?"

Jim walked to the door and opened it. "Yes, Cat, I'm OK," he said.

She threw her arms around him and kissed him and said, "I was so worried. I was afraid something would happen to you."

"I'm all right, Cat," he said, as he kissed her. "Now, run along and let Ted and me finish our report. I'll talk to you later." Then he shut the door and she returned to the sofa where Mark was lying.

"See, I told you she would check on you if you gave her a chance," Ted said.

When Cat walked over to the sofa where Mark was, she asked, "Mark, would you like a Coke or something?"

"Yes, I would love a Coke," he answered.

When she brought him the Coke, she asked if there was anything else he needed.

"Yes, I told you. I could use a little TLC," he answered. "That would help a lot."

"You need to call Jenny, if that's what you need," Cat answered.

"That's a good idea, Cat," he answered. "I think I will."

When he called, Jenny, she said that she would come as soon as she could get away. Soon, Jenny knocked on the door and Cat let her in and led her to where Mark was lying on the sofa.

"Hi, Mark," she said. "What happened to you?"

"Hi, Jenny, it's a long story," Mark answered. "I'm glad you came."

Then Jenny bent over and gave him a kiss. Mark pulled her down and kissed her again.

"I need some TLC, Jenny," Mark said. "Cat wouldn't give it to me. How about you?"

"I'm here, aren't I?" she asked.

Cat walked off to let them have some privacy. She went into the kitchen to see if Barbara was preparing dinner.

"Barbara, there will be another one for dinner," Cat said when she found Barbara busily preparing a meal. "Jenny just arrived."

"Thanks for letting me know," Barbara replied. "What about Ted and the other men?"

"I don't know," Cat said. "When Jim and Ted come out of Jim's office, I'll ask him."

When Cat asked Jim, he said that Ted and some of the men would stay for dinner and then they would go to the barracks to spend the night. The men had gone into town, but returned to eat and as soon as they had eaten, they left.

Barbara fixed Mark a plate and Jenny took it into the den and helped him eat. Cat thought that Mark must be happy, since Jenny was truly giving him some special TLC.

After dinner, Jim said that he was tired and was going upstairs. "Cat, do you want to come, too?" he asked.

"Sure, I'll be up in a few minutes," Cat answered. "I just want to get Jenny settled." Then she turned to Jenny and said, "Jenny, you can sleep in the room you had before. You will be staying tonight, won't you?"

"I didn't come prepared to stay, but I guess that would be a good idea," Jenny replied. "Thanks."

Then Cat went upstairs. Jim had already undressed, but was lying on top of the covers. "Come here, Cat," he said. Then he made love to her.

The next morning after breakfast, Jim told Cat, "I'm going into town. Do you want to come along?"

"Yes, of course," she said, as she ran upstairs to get a jacket and her purse. "What about Mark?" she asked as they were getting ready to go.

"Ted's here. He can take care of him, if Jenny has to leave," Jim said. "Mark, Cat and I are going downtown. We'll be back shortly. Ted is here if Jenny leaves. I told him to give you some TLC while we were gone."

"That's funny, Jim," Mark said sarcastically. "I think Jenny will give me enough to do me until you and Cat get back."

When Jim pulled up in front of the FSC building, Cat wondered why he had let her go with him, if he was going to see the Director.

He helped her out of the car and led her to the Director's office. "Director Halbert, you remember my wife, Cat, uh, Catherine, don't you?"

"Yes, I do. Hello, Mrs. Ryan," he said.

"Sir," Jim began. "Cat has recently become a member of my unit, as you know.

She has had some training, but I would like for her to have some extensive training. Can that be arranged?"

"Yes, of course," Director Halbert said. "As a matter of fact, I have four other recruits who are waiting for training. There are three males and one female, so she would fit right in with them. Do you want to do the training or do I need to get another trainer?"

"I would prefer that you have someone else do the training. Sometimes my wife doesn't like to do as I say."

"I know how that is," Director Halbert said. "I have a wife, too. I'll see if I can get Tony Michaels. He's one of the best. I'll set it up to start Monday for two weeks. How does that sound?"

"That sounds great," Jim answered. "My unit is down for a

while, anyway. That'll give them time to recuperate before I take another assignment. I want to observe the training, though. Do you mind?"

"No, I don't mind," the Director said. "You may even have some input."

"OK, it's set then," Jim said. "We'll be here at 8:00 a.m. Monday."

As they were leaving the building, Cat said, "Thanks, Jim. I'll try to make you proud. I'll get to be a great asset for your team."

"I know you will, Cat," he answered. "I've always been proud of you. The only reason I don't let you do things I know you can do, is because I want to keep you safe. I hope you can understand that. It's because I love you so much. Do you understand?"

"Yes, Jim," Cat replied. "I understand. I love you, too, but I know I can't keep you from doing dangerous things. I know that's your job and you have to do what you have to do. I still can hardly stand it when I know you're in danger, though. You'll just have to do like I do, and depend on God to keep me safe when you're not there to protect me."

"Yes, I know, Cat," he said. "But I want to be the one to protect you."

When they arrived back at home, Jenny was ready to leave.

"I'm glad you're finally here," she said. "I have to go. My Commander called and said he needs me on an assignment."

So she kissed Mark and was gone.

"What did you do to her?" Cat asked Mark, after she was gone.

"I didn't do anything to her," he answered. "She just had to go."

"Well, I thought she said she was going to stay for a couple of days," Cat persisted.

"She did, but she had to go," Mark said again. "Looks like you'll have to take care of me after all."

"No, she won't, Mark," Jim said. "You're going to start getting up and doing for yourself, starting right now. Get up and start moving."

"But, Jim," Mark argued. "I'm injured. You didn't get up and do for yourself so soon after your injury."

"You're not hurt as bad as I was," Jim said, as he pulled Mark to his feet and handed him a pair of crutches, "and I wasn't injured because of anything I did wrong. Now get up and get started learning how to use these things. Where's Ted?"

"He's in your office," Mark said, as he tried to stand using the crutches. "Come, here, Cat, and let me lean on you," Mark said, as he fell back onto the sofa.

"No, Cat, let him do it on his own," Jim said, as Cat started to help Mark.

"Gee, Jim, you're awfully cranky today," Mark said, as he tried to stand again. This time he made it, but he was really wobbly.

"I'm not cranky, Mark," Jim said, as he headed toward his office. "I just want you to be ready when we get another assignment. Now start walking with those things. Cat, don't help him."

After Jim went into his office and closed the door, Mark sat back down on the sofa. "He's angry with me for going ahead without him, Cat. This is his way of getting back at me."

"I don't think so, Mark," Cat said. "I think he just really wants you to hurry up and get well. He needs you. After all, you are his Second-in-Command."

"You're right, Cat," Mark said. "I guess I should be in his office, too. Help me get up again."

So Cat helped him to his feet and he hobbled over and knocked on Jim's door.

"Who is it?" Jim asked.

"It's Mark, Jim. Let me in," he said.

Ted opened the door and Mark went on inside.

"Jim," Mark started. "I want to apologize for the way I've been acting. I know that I probably wouldn't have gotten injured if I had listened to you. I just wanted to be a big shot Commander while I had the chance.

"I even thought I could take Cat away from you. That was a

mistake. She doesn't have eyes for anyone but you. If you want to fire me, I'll accept it. I know I deserve it, but I wish you wouldn't. I really love working with you and I hope you'll accept my apology."

"Are you through?" Jim asked.

"Yes, I guess so," Mark answered.

"I accept your apology," Jim said. "I will not fire you because I need you, but if you ever try to take Cat away from me again, I'll have to kill you. Do I make myself clear?"

"Yes, Jim," Mark lowered his head and said humbly. "I promise I'll never try that again."

"You'll never try what again?" Jim asked.

"I'll never try to take your job or your wife again," Mark answered.

"I accept your apology," Jim said. "Some day you may get my job when I retire, but you will never get my wife. Now, sit down. I need to brief you and Ted on some things."

Ted just sat back and thanked God that he wasn't on the receiving end of Jim's wrath. He had been with Jim long enough to know how protective he was of his job and his wife. He also knew that if Mark had continued to pursue Cat, there probably would have been some blood shed. He was glad that Mark had apologized. Now maybe everything would get back to normal.

"The Director is arranging a two-week training class for anyone who needs some extensive training," Jim said. "I'm going to take Cat to it. Do either of you know anyone who needs additional training?"

"No, I don't," Ted said. "All of my guys are pretty good at what they do. I think that's a good idea taking Cat, though."

"I don't know of anyone either, unless you think I might need some more training," Mark said sarcastically.

"No, Mark," Jim answered. "You just need to use the training you have already had."

When Jim finished briefing them on his plans, Ted said he was going to spend the night in the barracks with his men. They wanted to stay in the barracks because they felt they would be more at ease, so Ted said he would stay there with them.

After he had gone, Jim closed his office door and asked, "What happened with you and Jenny?" I thought you two hit it off really well."

"She didn't like the fact that I was using her," Mark answered.

"What do you mean using her?" Jim asked.

"I think you know what I mean, Jim," Mark answered. "I thought I made it plain enough."

"You mean how you feel about Cat?"

Mark didn't answer Jim's question. He just sat there in silence.

"Well, I feel sorry for you, Mark, but like I said, you can't have her," Jim said. "You might as well find someone else and be happy with her. Maybe you do need to transfer to another unit. Would that help?"

"No, Jim, I don't want to transfer," Mark answered. "I'll just try to stay away from Cat as much as possible. I'll eventually find someone. Maybe Jenny and I will get back together. After I get my head straight. Will you be able to work with me knowing how I feel about Cat?"

"I told you, Mark. I can work with you as long as you stay away from my wife. If you try to take her away from me, I may have to kill you," Jim said without even batting an eyelash. "Now, if you can work with me under those circumstances, I can work with you. After all, you've been a great partner. Now, I think I'll go upstairs. Do you want to go up or do you want to sleep on the sofa?"

"I think I'll just stay down here tonight," Mark answered. "I'll tackle the stairs tomorrow."

CHAPTER 9

On Monday morning, Cat awoke ready to go. She was excited about starting her training. She hurriedly dressed and ran downstairs. She ate her breakfast as fast as she could and urged Jim to hurry and finish so they could leave.

At the training facility, she was introduced to the other trainees. Cassidy Love was the other female in the class. She and Cat hit it off right at the start.

Tony Michaels introduced himself and asked each trainee to introduce themselves and tell to what unit they belonged. When Cat introduced herself, she said that she was in Jim Ryan's unit. Everyone was impressed. They had all heard about Jim Ryan and his unit; they were legendary. Cassidy was especially interested in the fact that Cat was a member of Jim's unit. She had been wanting to meet him ever since she first heard about him. After the introductions, Tony got right into the training.

Cat climbed rock walls and fences. She crawled through rain and mud. She learned how to open locks and how to enter buildings without being seen. She learned how to shoot different weapons. By the end of the day, every muscle in her body ached and she was covered in mud, but she was happy. When Jim came down to pick her up, he said, "If I didn't know it was you, Cat, I wouldn't have recognized you. How did you like your first day?"

"It was great," Cat said enthusiastically. "I loved every minute of it. I'm sore from the top of my head to the bottom of my feet, but I'm happy. I think I did well today."

"I think you did, too," Jim said. "I'm proud of you."

When Cassidy Love, a beautiful blonde with a figure that would stop a freight train, walked up, Cat introduced her. "Jim, this is my partner, Cassidy Love. Cassidy, this is my husband, Jim Ryan."

"Wow," Cassidy said. "Jim Ryan is your husband? You're so lucky. I've heard about Jim Ryan; I think everyone has. You're my hero, Jim."

Jim was flattered by Cassidy's words and could hardly take his eyes off of her. He was smitten with her. Cassidy noticed and started to flirt with Jim.

"Don't give him the big head, Cassidy," Cat said. "He's already conceited enough."

"I don't understand why I would be your hero, Cassidy," Jim said, as he turned red. "I just do my job like every other agent does."

"Yes, but you do it so much better than anyone, else," Cassidy said, as she leaned closer to Jim and touched his arm.

Jim was uncomfortable with Cassidy's touch, but he liked her attention.

"Cat, are you ready to go home?" Jim asked, feeling that he needed to get away from the effect Cassidy had on him.

"Yes, I'm so tired," Cat answered. "I can hardly wait to get into the shower."

When they arrived back at the cabin, Cat ran up the stairs and right into the shower. When she finished showering, the soreness had crept up into her muscles and she was slower going down the stairs than she had been going up them.

Barbara had dinner ready, so Cat joined everyone at the table. After Jim said a blessing on the meal, everyone dug into their food. Cat was starving, so it didn't take her very long to finish.

Mark had made it to the table, with the aid of his crutches. Ted and the other men were there, also, so there was a table full of people. After the initial silence when everyone was eating, they began talking. Jim said, "Everyone, I want to make an announcement. Cat made it through her first day of training. I'm really proud of her. She did really well."

Everyone clapped and said, "Way to go, Cat."

She was beaming. Jim didn't praise her often and she was eating it up.

About 8:00 p.m., Cat said, "I'm tired. I think I'll go on up to bed."

"I'll go with you. Mark are you going upstairs tonight?" Jim asked.

"No, I think I'll stay down here again," Mark answered. "I'm not quite ready to tackle the stairs yet."

Jim asked Ted if he was staying there too, and he said that he was going back to the barracks with the men.

In the bedroom, after Cat was ready for bed, she told Jim thanks for the kind words of praise. "I think that was the first time you've ever said anything good about something I've done," she said.

"Oh, is that so," Jim said, as he pulled her to him. "I should have told you what a good kisser you are; you're the best," he said, as he kissed her. "You're a really good bed partner, especially on cold nights," he said, as he kissed her neck. "Um, you're so delicious," he said, as he nibbled her ear. "I can think of lots of things that you're good at," he said, as he continued kissing her. "I'm sorry that I've never told you that before."

"Oh, Jim, that wasn't what I meant," she said, "but I'm glad you think so."

"You know I think so," he said, as he found her lips and made passionate love to her.

The next morning, Cat was up and ready to go again, even though every muscle in her body ached. She hurried Jim down to breakfast and out the door. He wanted to give some last-minute instructions to Ted, but he figured that Ted knew what to do anyway, so it didn't matter.

At the training session, Tony started the trainees on encoding and decoding. They learned how to interpret and how to crack different codes. Then it was back to the field again for some endurance training. Cat and Cassidy learned how to be good partners. They learned how to anticipate their partner's move. They did so well, they almost worked in unison. Tony even commented on how well they worked together. By the end of the second week, Cat and Cassidy were such good partners, they seemed to work as one individual.

On the last day of training, they paired off in teams of two and Tony gave them assignments. Cat and Cassidy won several awards, some as a team and some as individuals.

When Jim came down to pick up Cat, he told her how proud he was of her. He had been watching every day and was not only impressed with Cat, but had found Cassidy intriguing. Cat was happier than she had been for a long time. She basked in Jim's praise.

"Do you think we could get Cassidy to transfer to our unit?" Jim asked Cat.

"I don't know, Jim, you'll just have to ask her," Cat said.

When Cassidy walked up, Cat asked, "Cassidy, did I introduce you to my husband, Jim?"

"Yes, you did," she answered. "You're so lucky to have him. He's a doll. He's even handsomer that I was told."

"Thanks, Cassidy, I think so, too," Cat answered, feeling a little miffed that Cassidy would openly flirt with Jim.

"Cassidy, you and Cat work so well together, I was wondering if you would consider becoming a member of my unit?" Jim asked.

"Yes, I would love to work with THE Jim Ryan and your team," Cassidy answered enthusiastically. "Who wouldn't want to be on your team?" she said, as she got closer to Jim and touched his arm again. "You would have to OK it with my Commander, though."

"Who is your Commander?" Jim asked.

"Don Gardner," Cassidy answered. "Here he comes now."

Cassidy introduced Don to Cat and Jim, then Don said, "Wow. You're the great Jim Ryan. I'm pleased to meet you. I've heard a lot about you. I never thought I'd ever meet you, though."

"Thanks, but I don't deserve the title 'The great Jim Ryan'," Jim said. "I don't know who started that rumor. Don, I like the way Cat and Cassidy work together," Jim started slowly. "I'd like to see them work together on the same team."

"Yeah, so would I," Don answered. "They do make a good team, don't they?"

"Would you consider transferring Cassidy to my unit?" Jim asked.

"Hell, no," Don answered. "She's the only female I have on my team. I need her.

You transfer Cat to my team."

"I can't do that," Jim answered. "She's my wife and she stays where she is."

"Well, then, I guess they won't be working together, then," Don answered.

"Cassidy said she would like to work on my team. Cat and I want her to work with us," Jim persisted. He was determined to get Cassidy in his unit.

"Well, she can't go," Don said. "That's final."

"There must be someone on my team who I could trade to you for Cassidy," Jim said, not willing to let the matter drop.

"There is someone on your team that I would love to have," Don said.

"Who, just tell me and maybe we can make a deal," Jim was excited now. He couldn't think of anyone on his team that he wouldn't trade for Cassidy. He really wanted her.

"Ted Ames," Don said. "I want Ted Ames."

"Ted? You want Ted?" Jim's excitement suddenly dropped. "You can't have Ted. He's my right-hand man. I'd be lost without Ted."

"That's the deal," Don answered. "I get Ted, you get Cassidy. Take it or leave it."

Jim just stood there for a while not saying anything. Cat held her breath. Jim couldn't seriously be thinking of trading Ted for Cassidy. Ted was like family. He was always there for Jim. All through his illness, he had been right at his side. There's no way Jim could even consider trading Ted to Don, not even for Cassidy.

"I'll have to think about it," Jim said slowly. "I'll have to talk to Ted and see what he says. I'll get back to you."

"Suit yourself," Don said. "That's the deal; the only deal." Then he and Cassidy walked off.

"No, Jim," Cat said surprised that Jim would even think of trading Ted. "You can't even think of asking Ted a thing like that. How could you even consider it?"

"It's not your decision to make, Cat," Jim said, angry that she was once again questioning his authority.

"Jim, please, don't even ask Ted," Cat pleaded. "You'll hurt his feelings. You know how he feels about you. You would crush him. Please don't do it."

"Cat, I said for you to stay out of it," Jim said. "I need Cassidy. If I have to give Ted up, then so be it."

"Why? Why do you need Cassidy?" Cat asked.

"For you," Jim lied. "To be your partner."

"I don't need her if you're going to sacrifice Ted to get her."

"That's enough, Cat," Jim said, as they got to the car. "Just drop it. I'll handle it however I see fit. Don't question my authority again."

Cat wanted to say more, but she could see the determined set to Jim's jaw and she decided it would do no good to argue anymore. Jim was going to do what he wanted to do and she wasn't going to change his mind. There had to be some other reason Jim wanted Cassidy on his team. Cat didn't want to think on it too much. She was afraid of what she might discover.

When they arrived at the cabin, as usual, Barbara had a delicious dinner prepared and most of the team were there. Mark was beginning to get around a lot better, so he sat at the table with the others. Jim said the blessing on the food and, as usual, they all ate with gusto.

After the meal, Jim asked Ted to go into his office with him. Cat caught Jim's sleeve and said, "Jim, please don't." Jim just shook her hand off and proceeded to his office, followed by Ted.

"Ted," Jim started slowly. "Do you like working on my team?"

"Of course I do, Jim," Ted answered. "I thought you knew that."

"Have you ever thought about working on someone else's team?" Jim asked.

"Of course not, Jim," Ted answered. "What are you getting at?"

"I just wondered if you ever thought about working with someone else," Jim said.

"Are you unhappy with my work?" Ted asked. "Have I done something wrong?"

"No, of course not, Ted," Jim said. "Outside of Mark, you're the best man I have."

"Then why would you ask if I want to work with someone else?" Ted asked. "If you think I have designs on Cat, forget it. I'm not like Mark. I would never try to come between you and your wife."

"No, Ted, it isn't that," Jim said. "I know you wouldn't try to take Cat away from me like Mark did."

"What then? Why are you asking me this?" Ted asked.

"Because another Commander said that he would like to have you on his team,"

Jim said cautiously. "I told him I would ask you."

"Who is this other Commander?" Ted asked.

"Don Gardner," Jim said flatly.

"Don Gardner?" Ted was incredulous. "He's a slob. He's an egotist and a braggart. I wouldn't work for him if he was the last Commander in the whole Commission. Why would you even ask me if I would want to work with him? Would you want to work with him?"

"I'm sorry, Ted," Jim said dejectedly. "I shouldn't have even asked you."

"Why would you ask me?" Ted wanted to know. "I know you have a reason for asking me. We've been together for 15 years. I think

I know you even better than you know yourself. Tell me the real reason you asked me if I wanted to work for Gardner."

"He has someone that I want," Jim said slowly.

"Who? Who would you want over me?" Ted was about to cry. He had been deeply hurt.

"It doesn't matter now," Jim answered.

"Yes, it does matter," Ted said. "I want to know. I deserve to know who it is that you think would be more valuable to you than I am."

Jim took a deep breath and said, "It's a female, Cassidy Love. She and Cat worked so well together during training, I just wanted to get her for Cat's partner."

"Cat doesn't need someone else for her partner," Ted said. "Any of your men would have been honored to be her partner. You know how we all feel about Cat. She would have been well protected. I think you had another reason for wanting that girl.

You've got the best girl in the whole world. Why would you even want to jeopardize that?"

"You don't understand, Ted," Jim answered. "You should see them work together. It's amazing. There's two of them, but they work as one."

"I know you, Jim," Ted said. "Like I said, I think you have an ulterior motive for wanting this girl. I think you had better look at your reason for wanting her and consider what you're about to get yourself into."

With that, Ted headed for the door. "I might have to find another unit after this, but it won't be with Don Gardner," he said. Then he walked into the den, called his men and said he was ready to go.

Jim stood looking at the open door until Cat came in and shut the door behind her.

"It didn't go well, did it?" she asked.

"No, it didn't," Jim said. "I should have listened to you. My team is falling apart, Cat, and it's all my own stupid fault."

Cat came over to Jim and massaged his neck. "It's not your fault so much, Jim. Things just happen. You've had a lot happen to you lately. Maybe we need to take a vacation and go away for a few days. Maybe you came back to work too soon."

"Maybe you're right, Cat," Jim said, as he sat down at his desk. "Things are really in a mess right now. Even when I think I'm doing the right thing, it turns out to be wrong."

"I don't need Cassidy, Jim," Cat said. "It might have been nice to have worked with her, but not by sacrificing Ted."

"You care a lot about Ted, don't you, Cat?" Jim asked.

"Yes, I do," Cat answered.

"He cares about you, too," Jim answered.

"He cares about you, too, Jim, but I think now he probably doesn't care as much as he did. You shouldn't have done that to him," Cat said.

"I know that, now, Cat, but it's too late to do anything about it now," Jim said. "I'm sorry."

"I'm not the one you need to apologize to, Jim," Cat said.

"I know, Cat. I need to apologize to Ted, but I need to apologize to you, too. I was infatuated with Cassidy and I let it get to me. I'm sorry I even thought about Cassidy that way. I'm going upstairs. Did I tell you how proud I am of you? You really made me proud, today. I'm sorry I ruined it by making Ted mad. I'll see you upstairs," Jim said, as he walked out the door and left it open for Cat to follow.

When Cat came into the bedroom, Jim was lying on the bed still fully clothed.

"You know, Cat, I let Cassidy's adoration go to my head. I've never been anyone's hero before. I let it clog my thinking. I haven't been thinking straight ever since I met her."

"That's not right, Jim," Cat said, bending over and kissing him on the forehead. "You've always been my hero, ever since I was a little girl. No matter how you think you may have messed up, you're still my hero."

"Thanks, Cat," Jim said, as he pulled her down to him and

kissed her. "I needed that. Tomorrow, I'll have to make it up to Ted. Do you think he'll ever forgive me?"

"I don't know, Jim," Cat said, as she kissed him back. "I think you really hurt him. It may take a long time for him to get over it."

Jim lay awake a long time that night. Ted had said for him to examine his motive for wanting Cassidy on his team. Why had he wanted her so badly that he would jeopardize losing one of his best men. If he lost Ted, he would also be losing a good friend. He just hoped he hadn't lost his friendship forever. What was this attraction he had had for Cassidy? It had to be something more than the fact that she and Cat were so good together. Maybe he should thank God that things didn't work out. Maybe he did have an ulterior motive for wanting her on his team and God knew it and stopped it before it had gotten out of hand. Ted was right, Cat was the best thing that had ever happened to him. He certainly didn't want anything to come between Cat and him. Now, he would have to try and mend the breach between Ted and himself. He was afraid that that might take some doing. He realized now, that he had really hurt Ted. Tomorrow, he would have to try and make it up to Ted. He turned over and looked at his sleeping wife. He was amazed that someone as beautiful and wonderful as Cat could love him so much and his heart filled with love for her. Then he asked God to forgive him for what he almost did. Now, he was able to sleep.

CHAPTER 10

The next day was Saturday, and Ted didn't show up. He didn't come by on Sunday, either. Jim and Cat attended church services at the Landmark Baptist Church and Jim was hoping that Ted would come by after church, but he didn't.

On Monday morning, Jim went into his office to prepare for the new assignment. He usually had Ted or Mark there to help with the plans. Sometimes they were both there. Today, neither one came in, so Jim went into the den to see what Mark was doing. "Mark, are you all right?" Jim asked.

"I don't know, Jim," Mark said. "I started to get up and I got dizzy and fell back down. I think I had better just stay here for a while."

Cat was in the kitchen helping Barbara clean up. "Cat, will you come here for a minute?" Jim called from his office.

"Yes, Jim, what do you need?" she asked.

"Will you try to get hold of Ted?" Jim asked. "He should have been here by now. He may not answer if I call him."

"Sure, I will, but he may still be mad at you and not answer my call, either," Cat answered.

When she tried the first time, it just went into voicemail. She tried again and this time Ted answered on the fourth ring.

"Hello, Cat," Ted said. "Did His High-and-Mighty ask you to call me?"

"Yes, he did, Ted, but I wanted to call, anyway," Cat said.

"Why didn't he call himself? Is he too important to stoop that low to call me himself?" Ted asked sarcastically.

"He would have, but he didn't think you would have answered," Cat said.

"He's probably right," Ted said. "I guess he wants to know where I am. Tell him I'm looking for another unit."

"Ted, I know you're hurt," Cat started. "I would be, too, but please don't do this. You're not only hurting Jim, you're hurting the unit, also. Don't you know we need you? You're just like part of our family. If you leave, there'll be a hole where you were and no one will be able to fill it."

"Jim doesn't think so," Ted said. "He thinks Cassidy can fill my hole. You better watch out, Cat, you might be next. Maybe he thinks she can fill your hole, too."

"Ted, you're just being mean, now," Cat said, hurt at the sting of Ted's words.

"I'm sorry, Cat," Ted said. "I shouldn't take it out on you. I've been with Jim for 15 years. I've been his right-hand man for most of those years, and he's ready to dump me for a girl like Cassidy."

"Please come in and let's talk about it," Cat pleaded. "I know Jim is sorry. Come, let him make it up to you."

"OK, Cat, for you, I might come in," Ted said. "If I do come in, it won't be for Jim. I'm through going out of my way to please him."

About an hour later, Ted knocked on the door. Cat let him in and gave him a big hug. "I'm so glad you decided to come, Ted. Jim's in his office. Why don't you go on in?"

"I want to talk to you first," Ted said. "If I was you, I'd watch out for that Cassidy person. I think Jim had an ulterior motive for wanting her on his team and I don't think it was because you and she work so well together."

"It's OK, Ted," Cat said, as she led Ted to Jim's office. "I'm not worried. Jim belongs to me. He always has been and he always will be mine. Just like I'm his and I always will be," Cat said, with more confidence than she was feeling right then.

"Thanks for the warning, anyway," Cat continued. "Now, you go in there and let Jim apologize to you. I want to see you two be friends again. Please accept his apology."

She knocked on Jim's door and when he opened it, Jim grabbed Ted's hand and pulled him into his office and closed the door.

"I want to apologize to you, Ted," Jim began. "I know I was wrong. I just thought I wanted Cassidy on my team. I found out that I would have to pay a bigger price for her than I was willing to pay. I almost risked losing my wife, as well as my right-hand man. Thank you for straightening me out before I made a mistake that I could never correct."

"I accept your apology, Jim," Ted said. "Don't ever let it happen again, though. The next time, you might not be so lucky. Do you have your mind straight, now? If not, you're still treading on dangerous ground."

"I lost my head for a while, but now I think I'm thinking more clearly," Jim said. "Thanks, again, for heading me in the right direction."

"You just remember that, if you're ever tempted again," Ted said. "You've got the best wife any man could ever have and you risked losing her for what?"

"OK, Ted," Jim was ready to change the subject. "I get your point. I'm OK now. Let's just change the subject. Are you ready to work with me on a new assignment or not?"

"Yes, Jim," Ted said. "If you promise me this won't happen again."

"I can't make that a promise, but I'm sure it will never happen again," Jim said.

"Just see that it doesn't," Ted said.

Since that was settled, Jim and Ted were ready to get back to work and make plans for the new assignment. Then the phone rang. "Hey, Ryan. This is Don Gardner," he said, when Jim answered. "I thought you were going to call me this morning."

"I can't make a deal with you, Gardner," Jim answered. "Ted doesn't want to transfer, so the deal is off."

"Well, I'll take your wife, then," Gardner answered. "She would be an even better trade. You still want Cassidy, don't you?"

"No, I changed my mind," Jim answered. "I told you my wife isn't for sale. Forget it. I don't want Cassidy anymore."

"Well, she still wants to transfer to your unit. You never should have said anything about her transferring to your unit, if you were going to change your mind. She was happy with me until you told her you wanted her. Now, all she talks about is transferring to your team."

"Tell her I'm sorry, but we couldn't make a deal," Jim said. "I'm sorry I made her dissatisfied with you. She'll probably get over it soon."

"Yeah, like hell she will," Gardner said. "You'll regret not taking her, Ryan. Believe me you will."

Two weeks later, the Commissioner had an awards banquet for the winners of the training event. Since Cat was one of the winners, Jim and his unit were invited to attend.

Everyone in the unit wanted to go and see Cat receive her award, but Jim said someone had to stay and man the office. Since Mark was still having a little trouble getting around, he was elected to be the one to stay. He asked Ted to take a picture of him with Cat and Jim before they left, though.

"Be sure and take a video for me, also, so I can see Cat getting her award," Mark said, as he headed for Jim's office.

There was a large crowd at the banquet and everyone was standing around talking. There was so much noise, you could hardly hear anything. Jim and Cat were visiting with Director Halbert, when Cat saw Cassidy approaching them. She nudged Jim and nodded in Cassidy's direction. Jim sighed and prepared for an ugly scene.

"Well, hello, Cat, Jim," she said. "Fancy meeting you here. I would've thought you would be afraid of running into me and you would've stayed away."

"Look, Cassidy," Jim said, as he caught her arm and pulled her over to the side. "Please don't make a scene here. You know I had no option, but to tell you to forget the transfer."

"Oh, you had an option all right," Cassidy answered. "You just wouldn't take it."

"I wasn't about to trade Cat for you," Jim answered. "That would've been defeating my purpose, anyway. I wanted you and Cat to work together."

"Oh, really. I was under the impression that you wanted me for yourself," Cassidy said, as she ran her hand up and down Jim's arm.

Jim pulled away from her and said, "I guess both of us were wrong, then. There's no way I would have jeopardized my marriage for you."

Cassidy began to get mad and started to say something else, but Cat had finally excused herself from the Director and headed toward them.

As Cat walked up, Jim said, "I see someone I need to talk to." Then he hurried away and left Cat to cope with Cassidy.

"Cat, your husband thinks he's through with me," she said with an evil look toward Jim's back. "He's wrong, though. When I set out to get something or someone, I don't stop until I get it."

"Please, Cassidy," Cat begged. "Don't cause trouble for Jim. He's had enough trouble lately. If you cause him trouble, it'll cause trouble for the whole unit."

"You're such a wimp, Cat," Cassidy sneered. "You don't even deserve a man like Jim Ryan. How did you ever snare him anyway?"

"I love him and he loves me," Cat said, trying not to show Cassidy how hurt she was at her sharp words.

"I bet I could get him in bed in nothing flat," Cassidy said. "Then you'd see how much he loves you."

"Cassidy, you leave my husband alone," Cat said through

clenched teeth. "You'll wish you'd never caused him any trouble if you don't."

"We'll see who causes who trouble," Cassidy said. "I won't keep him, though. I have a husband who worships me. I'll just have some fun with Jim and then you can have him back." Then she walked away.

"You leave my husband alone," Cat said to Cassidy's retreating back.

Then the Director asked for everyone's attention. "Would you please take your seats?" he asked. "The food is ready to be served. I have asked Commander Jim Ryan to bless the food before we eat. Jim, please begin."

Jim said the blessing on the food and then he joined Cat and the others at the table that had been reserved for Jim's unit.

When Jim looked at Cat, he saw tears in her eyes. He took her hand and squeezed it. Then he mouthed the words, "I love you."

Cat smiled and did the same to Jim, but she really didn't feel like smiling. She just hoped that Cassidy didn't follow through with her threat.

After the meal, Director Halbert had the honor of handing out the certificates. As he called the names of the trainees, they filed across the stage and received their awards.

"Catherine Ryan, with Jim Ryan's Unit, took first place in five of the eight events in which she participated. I know Jim's unit must be very proud of her."

As she walked across the stage to receive her award, Jim and the whole unit stood and applauded. They also remembered to take the video for Mark.

"It looks like they're very proud of her," Director Halbert said.

"Last, but not least is Cassidy Love, with Don Gardner's Unit. She took the other three first place awards that Catherine didn't take. The whole Commission is very proud of our new female trainees. I know that they'll make their units succeed in each assignment they undertake. Now let's have a big hand for all of the trainees."

Everyone stood and applauded for several minutes. Cat would have been very happy if Cassidy hadn't ruined it for her. She just hoped that Cassidy didn't follow through with her threat.

A few days later, Jim asked Cat if she wanted to go to town with him. He said he had some shopping he needed to do. Cat said that there were a few things she needed, too, so they left Mark in charge of the office again and headed downtown.

After Jim did his shopping, Cat said she would like to shop for a new dress, so they went to the dress shop. Cat picked out several dresses she wanted to try on and headed to the fitting room.

Jim was looking at some dresses on a nearby dress rack when someone put her arms around his waist. He thought it was Cat, so he smiled and turned around to face Cassidy Love.

"Hello, Jim Ryan," she said. "What are you doing in a dress shop? Where's Cat? Did she let you off your leash?"

"Cat's around somewhere," Jim said, as he extricated himself from her embrace and backed away from her. "No, she didn't 'let me off my leash' as you put it. She doesn't have me on a leash," he said angrily.

"Well, it sure seems like it," Cassidy said, as she caressed his arm. "Every time I see you, she isn't very far away."

Jim took Cassidy's hand and pushed it away from his arm. Then he stepped back another step. "Look, Cassidy. I don't want any trouble with you," he said. "I have a happy marriage and I don't need you to mess it up."

"You want me, Jim," she said, as she took a step toward him. "I can see it in your eyes."

"No, Cassidy," he said, taking another step backward and bumping into the dress rack. "I just want you to leave us alone. I made a mistake when I asked you to transfer to my unit. Forget that I ever did that and just go on with your life."

"No, Jim," she said, as she pulled him to her and kissed him hard on the lips. "No, I won't leave you alone. Not until I get what I want."

"What do you want, Cassidy?" Jim asked, as he wiped his mouth on the back of his hand.

"I want you, Jim Ryan," she said. "I want to tell everyone that I took down the famous Jim Ryan."

Jim sighed and pushed her away from him again. "I wouldn't have you if you were the last woman on earth," Jim said. "Now, leave me the hell alone."

"You'll be sorry you said that, Jim Ryan," Cassidy said angrily. Then she slapped him and walked away. Cat was just coming out of the dressing room when she saw Cassidy slap Jim and walk away.

"What was that all about?" Cat asked, as she walked up to Jim.

"Nothing," he said, as he wiped his lips again. "Come on let's get out of here."

"What about my dress?" Cat asked.

"You can get it some other time," he said, as he took her arm and led her to the exit.

Cat hung the dress she had in her hand on the rack and followed Jim out of the shop. When they were in the car headed home, Cat asked, "What did she say to you that made you so mad?"

"It's nothing, Cat," he said angrily. "Just forget it. I'm sorry I ever laid eyes on that woman."

After that incident, whenever Jim went to town, Cassidy would find him. It seemed as if she was stalking him. He finally decided that he was going to put an end to it. He caught her by the arm and said, "Cassidy, I'm tired of this. Stop following me around. I'm not going to bed with you and that's final. If you persist, I'm going to have you arrested. Now, leave me alone."

Cassidy became very angry and said, "I'll have you arrested first. If I tell them you molested me, they'll believe me. If you don't go to bed with me, I'll cause you more trouble than you can imagine. I'll have your job. I can do it, too. You know I can. Either you come to me or I'll press charges against you."

"Do it then," Jim said angrily. "No one will believe you. Why would I want you when I have Cat?"

"You'll find out," Cassidy said, as she stormed out of the store. "You'll be sorry."

"I already am sorry," Jim said to her retreating back. "I'm sorrier than you'll ever know," Jim said to himself. "Please, God, just let this end. Please don't let me lose Cat because of it." Then he went to his car and sadly drove home.

The next week, as Jim was planning his unit's next assignment, Director Halbert called. "Jim, I'm sorry to have to tell you this, but you're going to have to go before the Review Board again. Cassidy Love has filed charges against you. Do you know anything about that?"

"Yes, Sir, I do," Jim answered. "They're totally false, though. You have to believe me, Sir. I didn't do any of the things she's accusing me of doing."

"If you didn't, then how do you know of what she's accusing you?" Director Halbert asked.

"Sir, she's been harassing me for some time now," Jim answered wearily. "She said if I didn't do as she said, she would file charges against me. Everything she's said is a lie. It's the other way around, Sir."

"Well, you'll have your chance to prove it," Director Halbert said. "I'm sorry, but I'll have to suspend you again until this matter is settled. Is Agent Fuller ready for active duty again?"

"Yes, Sir, Agent Fuller can take over as Commander," Jim answered. "I'll let him know, Sir."

"Thank you, Jim. I hope everything works out OK for you," Director Halbert said. "This has been a rough year for you hasn't it, Jim?'

"Yes, Sir. It has been one heck of a year," Jim answered.

Once again, Jim stood before the Review Board.

"Commander Ryan," the Commissioner began. "This is your third appearance in one year before the Review Board. What do you have to say for yourself?"

"That isn't fair, Sir," Jim answered. "The second time was due to an injury that I sustained while on the job. This time I have been falsely accused."

"You said that the second time was due to your injury," the Commissioner said.

"That's true, but there was a shooting incident, I recall. Was there not?"

"Yes, Sir," Jim answered. "It was an accidental shooting."

"I believe both incidents had something to do with your wife. Am I correct?"

"Yes, Sir, in a way," Jim answered.

"Now, this incident indirectly involves your wife, also. Is that not correct?"

"No, Sir. My wife has nothing to do with this," Jim could feel himself losing his temper. He had to make himself cool down. This was going to be hard enough without his losing his cool.

"We have already heard Agent Love's version. Now, we want to hear your version," the Commissioner said.

"OK," Jim began. "Cassidy Love and my wife, Catherine, were in training together. They worked so well together, that I asked Agent Love if she would like to transfer to my unit and work with Cat. She said she would if her Commander, Don Gardner, would agree to let her transfer. He didn't want to let her transfer at first, but agreed later, if one of my agents agreed to transfer to his unit to replace Agent Love. When my agent didn't agree to the transfer, I called the deal off. Agent Love got angry because she wanted to transfer anyway. So now she's just trying to get back at me by filing false charges against me."

"You're telling us that there was nothing sexual involved. Is that what you're saying?" the Commissioner asked.

"There was nothing sexual on my part, Sir," Jim answered. "Agent Love may have misunderstood my intentions. I only wanted her to transfer to work with my wife because they worked so well together."

"Commander Ryan, will you swear that you had no ulterior

motive in wanting Agent Love to transfer to your unit?" the Commissioner asked.

"Yes, Sir, I will," Jim answered.

"Let me read a statement made by one of your agents. This is from Agent Ted Ames. Do you want me to read what he has to say?" the Commissioner asked.

"That won't be necessary," Jim answered. "I believe I know what he had to say. He's angry because he was the one I was going to transfer."

"So you're saying that what Agent Ames has said is a lie?" the Commissioner asked.

"No, Sir. I didn't say that," Jim answered. "Agent Ames misunderstood my reason for wanting Agent Love to transfer to my unit. Now, he's angry that I would even consider transferring him, so he's just trying to cause trouble for me."

"Is that so?" the Commissioner asked. "Commander Ryan, you've had an exemplary career so far. You have never had any trouble within your unit. All of your men have worked together as smoothly as clockwork. Now, all of a sudden, you're telling me that one of your men, I think you call him your right-hand man, is just trying to cause you trouble because you want to transfer him. Is that what you're trying to say?"

"Yes, Sir," Jim said, as he bowed his head. He knew he was defeated. He just decided to give up. There was no longer any fight left in him.

"Commander Ryan, is your wife here?" the Commissioner asked.

"Yes, Sir, she is," Jim answered.

"Do you mind if we talk to her?" he asked.

"No, Sir, I don't mind," Jim answered. "She'll tell you the same thing I've already told you about Agent Love."

"Will you go out to the waiting area and send your wife in?" the Commissioner asked.

When Cat came into the room, the Commissioner asked

her to be seated. "You are Agent Catherine Ryan, I assume," the Commissioner asked after she was seated.

"Yes, Sir, I am," Cat answered.

"Do you understand why Commander Ryan is here today?" the Commissioner asked.

"Yes, Sir, I think so," Cat answered.

"Give us, then, your version of what took place between Commander Ryan and Agent Love," the Commissioner asked. "You do know Agent Love's charges, do you not?"

"Yes, Sir, I know what she said," Cat answered through clenched teeth.

"OK, start at the beginning and tell us what happened," the Commissioner said.

"Agent Love and I had a training class together," Cat began. "We really hit it off at first. We were working really well together. It was like we had been partners for years.

Then I made the mistake of introducing her to my husband, Jim Ryan. She acted like she had gone gaga over him. You know what I mean?"

When the Commissioner said he understood what she meant, Cat continued. "Anyway, she said she had heard about Jim and she had been wanting to meet him, because he was her hero. Jim didn't like to be called a hero, and he told her so. She still kept on about how great he was and that everyone knew the great Jim Ryan. She couldn't keep her hands off of him. I was sorry that I had introduced her to Jim.

"Jim thought that I would like to work with her, so he tried to get her transferred to his unit. I thought it was a bad idea, but I didn't say anything, because he thought he was doing the right thing. When the transfer didn't work out, I was really glad. Agent Love was furious, though. She said that she would get even with Jim for stopping the transfer.

"At the awards banquet, she bet me that she could get Jim to go to bed with her. Can you imagine someone telling you that they would get your wife to go to bed with them?"

"No, Agent Ryan, I couldn't imagine that. You must have felt awful," the Commissioner said.

"Yes, Sir, I did," Cat continued. "After that, she flirted with Jim every time she saw him. I think she even made it a point to be wherever he was. She was always touching him and trying to get him to touch her. Believe me, Sir, I wanted to kill her myself. I know I shouldn't be saying this to you, but I did. I would be happy to see something bad happen to her. She's the only person I have ever said that about. She's just trying to ruin Jim's career and his life. I think that she feels that if she can't have him, then she'll ruin him." Cat stopped speaking and took a deep breath.

"Are you finished, Agent Ryan?" the Commissioner asked.

"Yes Sir, that's all I can think of right now," Cat answered.

"You may go, then. Tell Commander Ryan to wait in the waiting area until I call him again," the Commissioner said, as he escorted Cat to the door and shut it behind her.

Cat went over and sat next to Jim. He took her hand and squeezed it. "I'm sorry to have put you through this, Cat. If you want to leave me after this, I'll understand."

"I could never leave you, Jim," Cat said with tears in her eyes. "I love you too much. I don't think there's anything you could do to change that. I just hate that we have to be going through this. I just pray that God will work it out, somehow."

Jim held her to his chest and kissed her. "I'm so glad I have you, Cat. I can never make it up to you, but I'll try. I don't deserve you, I know, but I love you and I'm so sorry that I put you through this."

Then they sat in silence. The only sound was a sniffle now and then from Cat. She tried to cry as softly as she could, but she had to sniffle every now and then. The time dragged by slowly and soon it had been two hours. Jim stood up and began pacing. "What's taking so long?" he asked. "Why can't they just get it over? I can't stand this waiting."

"I know," Cat answered. "This has been the hardest two hours of my life," she thought. "Will it ever end?"

Finally, someone came and told Jim he was wanted back in the Boardroom. He took Cat's hand and squeezed it before he followed the page into the room.

"Commander Ryan," the Commissioner started. "According to you and your wife, the charges against you are false. We have the statement from Agent Love and Agent Ames that dispute what you've said. We need to further review the evidence. You will remain on suspension until further notice. You are to have no connection with the missions assigned to your unit until further notice. Do I make myself clear?"

"Yes, Sir," Jim said. "I understand perfectly."

"Then you're dismissed until further notice. Please leave your badge at the desk on your way out. This hearing is adjourned."

Jim hurried out the door, threw his badge on the desk, grabbed Cat's hand and pulled her out the exit. He didn't say anything until they were in the car.

"I'm suspended until further notice," he said. "They took my badge. They told me I couldn't have any contact with my unit until they notified me. What have I done to us, Cat? What have I done?" He lay his head on the steering wheel and cried.

Cat wanted to comfort him, but she didn't know how. His job had been the most important thing in his life. Now what would he do. If he was dismissed because of Cassidy Love, it would be a terrible injustice. Oh, how she hated that woman. The only thing Cat knew to do was pray and she did pray. She poured out her anguish to the only One who could help her and Jim. She knew if anyone could save Jim's job and his reputation, it would have to be God.

"I can't go home right now, Cat," Jim said, as he sat up and started the car. "I can't face Ted. I know he had something to do with why they delayed making a decision today. Let's drive down to the lake. Is that OK with you?"

"Sure, Jim. Whatever you want," Cat said.

When they got to the lake, there were very few people there. There was a cold March wind blowing, so people didn't come to the lake on days like that. Jim wrapped his arms around Cat, as they walked to a vacant picnic table. He held her tight to keep her warm. For a few minutes they both looked out at the lake rippling in the wind and neither one wanted to break the silence.

After a while, Jim said, "Cat, I'm so sorry. I lost my head for a while, but I would never have been unfaithful to you. I still don't know why I did what I did. I love you more than anything in the whole world. I would never have wanted to hurt you like that. I can't stand to see you hurt. Can you ever forgive me?"

"Jim, I know you wouldn't have done anything to hurt me," Cat said. "Sometimes, we just do things and don't even realize we're doing them until it's too late. Maybe you thought you were doing the right thing. Maybe not, but both of us will have to pay the consequences. We'll get through it, though. With God's help, we'll get through it."

Cat lay her head on Jim's shoulder and cried. She couldn't stop crying. She cried until there were no more tears left for her to cry. Jim cried, too. He kissed her forehead. He kissed her cheeks. He kissed her tear-stained eyes. Finally, he kissed her lips.

"Cat, I meant it when I said you could leave if you want to go," he said. "I can't live without you, but I don't deserve you. If you feel you can't stay with me, I'll understand."

"Jim, I could never leave you," she said. "When we got married, I promised to love you till death would part us. I meant those vows that I made. There's no way I would leave you and let you face this alone. We'll come through it. Like the saying goes, 'What doesn't kill you, just makes you stronger.' We'll both come out of this stronger. You'll see. God will handle it. I know He will. We just have to believe that He will."

"I believe, Cat," Jim said. "If you believe it that much, then I believe, too. Come on, let's go home. I need to get you out of this cold before you freeze. I think I can face Ted now."

This time when he started the car, he had a brighter outlook. With God and Cat on his side, how could he lose. Yes, he knew there was a rough road ahead, but he had had rough times before and God had always gotten him out of them. He knew that eventually God would get him out of this mess. It may not be the way he would like for God to get him out, but he knew that God would eventually get him out. He still dreaded facing Ted, but at least he wouldn't have to work with him for a while. He may not ever work with him again. What would he do if he lost his job? Working for the FSC was all he knew. He started right out of high school. Would he be able to do something else? What about Cat? He had gotten her into his unit. What would happen to her? The Commissioner of the Review Board said he couldn't have any connection with his unit. Did that include Cat? Surely not. He certainly couldn't make it without her. What was he going to do? Well, he was almost home. He would find out how he felt about Ted soon.

CHAPTER 11

When Jim and Cat arrived at the cabin, Jim hesitated for a few minutes. "Cat, I can't face Ted. I feel like he sold me out," Jim said.

"You'll just have to forgive him, Jim," Cat said. "I'm sure he did what he felt was best for the unit. You know Ted has always been loyal to you and your unit. Even though he was hurt that you were going to trade him, I still think he's loyal to the unit."

"I don't know, Cat," Jim said. "It still hurts that he would sell me out even after that."

"Come on in. I'm getting cold standing out here," Cat said shivering.

As they entered the cabin, Mark and Ted wanted to know how the hearing went.

"Not good," Jim said. Then he turned on Ted and said, anger in his voice, "Thanks for your help, Ted."

"What do you mean 'thanks for your help'?" Ted asked.

"I mean just that," Jim said angrily. "If you hadn't given them that report, they might have found in my favor. Now, I'm suspended for no telling how long."

"I didn't give them any report, Jim," Ted said "I don't know what you're talking about. You know I would never betray you, even though you almost betrayed me."

"You mean they never asked you about why I wanted Cassidy in my unit?" Jim asked.

"No, why would they?" Ted asked. "Did you see a report from me?"

"No, I didn't see it. They just said they had a report," Jim answered.

"Well, if they had a report, it wasn't from me," Ted answered.

"Those sorry," Jim said angrily. "They asked if I wanted them to read it to me. They knew I would say no. I played right into their hands. I figured that you would have said something about Cassidy and me, so I didn't want to hear it. I just incriminated myself. Boy, have I really messed things up."

"It'll all work out, Jim," Ted said, as he put an arm around Jim's shoulders. "Surely they can see through someone like that. If she did it to you, she probably has done it to someone else. We just need to find someone who'll testify against her."

"This is my problem, Ted," Jim said. "I don't want you to get involved. You're already involved too much."

"You're our Commander, Jim," Ted said. "Whatever affects you affects us. That's what we're trained to do, find people. We can do it."

"I said stay out of it, Ted," Jim said. "Anyway, I'm not supposed to have any connection to my unit until further notice."

"No connection. What does that mean?" Mark asked.

"It means exactly what it says," Jim answered. "That means you either need to move the office to the FSC building or Cat and I have to leave for a while."

"Cat's part of the unit. How is that going to work?" Mark asked.

"Cat goes with me even if she is part of the unit. She's my wife. Wherever I go, she goes," Jim answered.

"But, Jim. I need her in the unit," Mark said. "With you and Cat both out, I'll be short handed. We have to go back to North Korea and I need all the help I can get."

"Cat isn't going," Jim said angrily. "If I don't go, she doesn't go. She goes nowhere without me."

"Jim, I've got to have her," Mark argued. "She's good. She

couldn't have won those awards, if she wasn't. I need her. You have to let her go."

"I said she doesn't go without me and that's final," Jim said.

"Jim, you know I'll protect her," Mark said. "I've been doing that for several years now. You've got to let her go."

"Protecting her here is a whole lot different than protecting her in North Korea," Jim said. "She can't go and that's final."

Then he stormed up the stairs and into their bedroom. Mark started to go after him, but Cat stopped him.

"Wait, Mark," she said. "Let him cool off for a little while, then I'll go talk to him."

"OK, but I need a decision soon," Mark said. "We'll have to leave early in the morning. Don Gardner and one of his teammates got themselves captured while they were on a rescue mission in North Korea again. The director gave us orders to go in and get them out."

"Don Gardner's team?" asked Cat. "Is Cassidy Love with them?"

"Yes, she is, Cat," Mark said hesitantly. "I didn't want to say anything in front of Jim. I knew he wouldn't let you go, if he knew she was there. After all, she's the reason for his suspension."

"If I do persuade him to let me go, he can't know it's Cassidy," Cat said. "Please don't say anything about her being one of them."

"Sure, Cat," Mark answered. "That's why I didn't say she was there."

After Cat thought enough time had elapsed for Jim to have cooled off, she went upstairs to talk to him. She knocked lightly on the door, and he told her to come in.

"Jim, you know I'm part of your unit. They need me. I really need to go with them," Cat said, as she sat down next to Jim on the bed.

"Cat, I have already lost the job I love. You're the only other thing in this world that I love. If I lose you, I might as well die. There'll be no reason for me to continue living," Jim said.

"I know how you feel, Jim, but you made me a part of your team.

Now, I'm committed to it. Mark needs me. I have to go with them tomorrow," Cat said, as she stroked his back and massaged his neck.

Jim took her hand and kissed it. "You really know how to win an argument with me, don't you?" he asked. "You know I'm just putty in your hands. What will I do, if something happens to you, Cat?"

"We just have to depend on God to take care of me and the team," Cat said. "What good is faith if you don't have to exercise it sometimes?" Cat asked.

"OK, Cat, go then." Jim gave a deep sigh and said, "I guess I'll just have to leave you in God's hands and trust that He'll bring you back safely to me."

While Cat and Jim were upstairs, Mark was on the telephone talking to Director Halbert.

"Director, I'm sure you know that Jim Ryan has been suspended and our team has been assigned the task of rescuing Don Gardner's team from North Korea," Mark began.

When the Director said he was aware of it, Mark continued. "I really need Jim to help with this assignment. Can't he at least go as an advisor?"

"The Board has made their decision, and I can't go against their wishes, Mark. You know I can't," Director Halbert said.

"Isn't there some way that Jim can go and just be an advisor? He won't have to participate in the rescue. He could just go with us to South Korea and help plan the rescue, but stay in South Korea, when we execute the plan. Sir, we really need him. You know what happened the last time we went to North Korea without Jim," Mark continued to argue.

"You're right, Mark. Maybe we can bend the rules a little. Let me talk to the Commissioner and see what he says. If he agrees, then Jim can go to South Korea and help with the plan, as you suggested, but remain in South Korea while you execute the plan."

Mark paced Jim's office waiting for a call from Director Halbert. Finally, after an hour, the phone rang. Mark grabbed it on the first ring.

"Mark, it took a lot of arguing and persuading, but I finally got the Board to see it your way. Jim can accompany you and the team to South Korea and help with the plan. He is not to go on the assignment with the team, though. You will be in command of this rescue. Do you understand?"

Mark said that he fully understood that Jim would not be allowed to accompany the team on the rescue mission, but that he was to accompany them to South Korea and help with the plan.

"Make sure that Jim understands, Mark," the Director sternly answered.

"Yes, Sir. I'm sure he will understand completely," Mark answered and hurriedly ended the call, so he could relay the message to Jim and Cat.

Mark hurried up the stairs and knocked loudly on their bedroom door.

"What is it, Mark?" Jim asked, wondering what was so important that Mark had rushed upstairs to tell him.

"Jim, I just finished talking to Director Halbert," Mark excitedly began. Then he told Jim and Cat what the Director had said.

"Good. I can at least go with you to South Korea. That will make me feel a little better," Jim said, as he gave a sigh of relief.

The next morning, everyone was up and ready to go by 5:00 a.m. Ted, Mark and Jim loaded the gear into the van and then told Cat they were ready to go.

"We'll pick the others up at the barracks as we go out," Ted said, as he walked toward the door.

After picking up the other team members, Ted drove them to the Little Rock AFB where a C17 was waiting to take them to Osan AB in South Korea.

After landing at Osan AB, the crew members rested for a couple of hours, then Mark borrowed the conference room and he and Jim began to make plans for the rescue.

Early the next morning, the unit was ready to attempt the rescue. As they headed toward the chopper, Jim took Cat into his arms and kissed her deeply. He didn't want to let her go, but he felt he had no choice. "I love you, Cat. Come back safely to me. I need you," he said, as he told her goodbye.

"Mark, Ted, I'm counting on you to keep her safe," Jim said. "If she doesn't come back, you better not come back, either."

"We'll get her back safely, Jim," Mark said more confidently than he felt. He remembered the last time he went on a mission without Jim. It was disastrous. He prayed that this mission would end differently.

When they got to the drop zone, Mark had an uneasy feeling. "Ted, I think they're waiting for us," he said. "I have a feeling that we're being watched. Stay close to Cat. Don't let her get separated from us."

"There's Don and Cassidy," Cat said pointing to a group of trees at the edge of the clearing where they landed.

"Wait," Mark shouted. "It's a trap. Get back to the chopper. Abort. Abort!"

They all ran for the helicopter, but were fired upon. Mark got a bullet in his back, but Cat helped him to the chopper. Ted and Bill were hit as they tried to get inside the helicopter.

"Go, go," yelled Mark. "Get out of here."

The helicopter was hit, but it managed to make it almost to the South Korean border. Then it nose-dived toward the ground. "We're going down," yelled Mark. "Everyone brace yourselves."

There was a terrible earth-shattering boom, as the helicopter hit the ground. Cat hit her head and blood began to pour into her eyes. She took a tissue out of her pocket and daubed at it as well as she could, but it continued to bleed.

"Mark, are you all right?" she asked.

"I'm hurt bad, Cat, and Ted's unconscious. See if you can get someone on the radio," Mark answered.

She tried, but got no answer. "Cat, try to get someone. I can't help you. I'm passing out," Mark said and then he was unconscious, too.

Cat could see the North Koreans searching for them. She was so scared, she began to pray. "God, please get us out of this, if possible."

Cat tried the radio again, praying that someone would answer this time. "Cat, is that you?" Jim answered, as he intercepted the radio call.

"Jim, we're in trouble," she cried, as soon as she heard Jim's voice. "They were waiting for us. They shot us down. We crashed and now they're coming for us. Mark's hurt bad and Ted's unconscious. I think the pilot's dead. Please get some help."

"Cat, give me your coordinates. Hurry," Jim said.

Cat found the coordinates as quickly as she could and read them off to Jim.

"Get someone quick, Jim," she said.

"Get someone, hell," Jim said, as he ran out the door. "I'm coming, Cat. Hold on."

"No, Jim, you can't come," Cat cried. "Get someone else."

"I'm coming, Cat," he said, calling over his shoulder, as he ran out onto the tarmac looking for a helicopter. "To hell with the Review Board." There were several choppers sitting there waiting for an assignment.

"Get me a chopper and a pilot as fast as you can. My team's down behind enemy lines," Jim shouted to a crew member.

One pilot walked out to see what Jim was yelling about. "Aren't you on suspension, Commander Ryan?" he asked.

"Yes, but I have to get to my team," he yelled. "If you don't fly me, I'll do it myself."

"I can't do that, Commander Ryan," the pilot said. "Not with you on suspension."

"Get out of my way, then. I'll fly it myself. I know how to fly," Jim said, as he shoved the pilot out of his way and headed for the helicopter.

"All right, if you're determined to go, I'll fly you," the pilot said. "I don't want you to crash my chopper."

They jumped into the helicopter and Jim gave the pilot the coordinates and they were off.

"My name's Greg Benson," the pilot said. "I've flown for you before. I don't know if you remember me or not."

"Yes, I remember you," Jim said. "You're a good pilot. I need a good pilot. My team, including my wife, were shot down by the North Koreans. The pilot didn't make it and my team members are all injured. The North Koreans know where they are and are on their way to pick them up. I need to get to them before the North Koreans do. Do you understand me?"

"Yes, Commander Ryan," he answered. "I completely understand."

Cat had gathered as many of the weapons as she could and had them close to her. She didn't intend to go down without a fight.

"Give me one, Cat," Mark said. "I'll try to stay conscious as long as I can. You can't hold them off by yourself."

"I won't be by myself, Mark," she said. "God will be with me. I'll hold them off as long as I can."

When they got within 100 yards of the helicopter, Cat had no other alternative, but to start shooting. Her practice on the firing range was paying off. She was giving them almost as much as they were giving her. Mark helped as long as he could, but soon passed out again.

"Please, Jim, hurry," she begged.

Just when she thought she was a goner, she heard another chopper. Gunfire from the chopper made her pursuers scatter.

"Come on, Mark. Wake up," she said, as she shook him back into consciousness.

"Jim's here. We have to hurry. They won't stay away for long. Help me with Ted."

Cat and Mark struggled with Ted and got him to the door. As the helicopter landed, Jim jumped out and ran to Cat. He grabbed Ted and helped Mark out. Cat jumped out of the downed chopper and ran behind Jim to the waiting helicopter.

As Cat expected, the North Koreans started running toward them again, firing as they ran. "Who else is here?" Jim asked Cat.

"Bill and Fred are in bad shape," she answered.

"You go get into the chopper," Jim said, as he climbed back into the downed helicopter. "I'll get the others."

Jim and the others barely made it to the helicopter before the North Koreans arrived. Greg took off almost before Jim could get inside and slam the door shut. The North Koreans fired at the helicopter and it took several hits, but it continued to fly.

As soon as they got back to the base in South Korea, they unloaded the injured and took them to the infirmary to be treated. Mark and Ted were both in pretty bad shape.

"Cat, you're bleeding," Jim said. He had just noticed that Cat had been injured, too. "Come on, let's get you taken care of, too."

"No, Jim," Cat said, as she pulled away from him. "We have to go back."

"You're not going back," Jim said, as he pulled her toward him. "You're hurt. You're going to the infirmary to be treated."

"Jim, listen to me," Cat pleaded. "It's Don and Cassidy. We saw them. They tried to get to us, but they were captured. You know what they'll do to them, now."

"You mean you risked your life and mine for Cassidy Love?" he said incredulously. "The person who ruined my life? The person who took my job away from me? That Cassidy Love? Is that who you want me to risk my life again for? No, Cat. No way. Let them torture and kill her for all I care. I say good riddance. You're not going back either. You're going into the infirmary and get treated for your injury," he said, as he tried to pull her toward the infirmary, but she stood her ground and wouldn't budge.

"Jim, you can't just let her die," Cat said.

"Why not?" Jim asked. "She threw me to the wolves. I'm not even supposed to be doing this. I've probably already gotten Greg into trouble. I'm not even supposed to get involved with my team. Cat, do you know what you're saying?"

"Yes, Jim, I know what I'm saying," Cat said. "I know what can happen if the Review Board finds out, which I'm sure they will. You and I will both be without a job, but we have to try to save her. You'll never forgive yourself if you don't try. I know you, Jim. You're not as heartless as you think you are. Now, let's find a good chopper and a pilot and go see if we can bring them home."

"Well, I'm already in trouble anyway, I might as well do something else. They can fire me only one time. You're going to get that injury taken care of while I find a pilot and a chopper. If you don't, I'm not going back," Jim said, as he pushed her toward the infirmary and started across the asphalt to find a helicopter that was in working order.

As soon as Cat had gotten her head bandaged, she was out the door looking for Jim. She found him standing next to a helicopter talking to Greg, the pilot.

"Cat, Greg has offered to take us back in," Jim said, as he put his arm around her and pulled her to him. "He said that he had already disobeyed orders once, so he might as well go. I guess he's like me. They can only fire you once. Isn't that right, Greg?"

"Sure, Commander Ryan," Greg said.

"Call me Jim," Jim answered. "Oh, this is my wife, Cat. In case you two haven't been formally introduced."

"Nice to meet you, Cat," Greg said. "Are you ready to go?"

"Yes, as soon as you are," Cat answered.

"We're ready; climb aboard," Greg said, as he helped Cat into the chopper.

As they neared the drop zone, Cat became nervous. "What am I doing?" she wondered. "This is insane. Not only am I causing more trouble for Jim, I am also causing Greg to get into trouble, too."

Then she had no more time to think. It was time to either do or die. There was no turning around now. She and Jim landed fairly close together. She watched as the helicopter became smaller and smaller. She took a deep breath, took her weapon in her hand and followed Jim toward the compound where they figured Cassidy and Don were being held.

"You stay here," Jim said, as he pushed her behind some bushes. "I'll go see if I can see where they are."

Jim was gone so long, that Cat was beginning to wonder if he had been captured. Then all of a sudden, there he was.

"I've spotted them, but it's going to be tough," Jim said. "They're heavily guarded and chained to the wall. There's only one way into the room and there are guards inside and outside. Cat, I don't see how we can get them without being captured ourselves."

"Would you do it if I was the one in there?" Cat asked.

"Of course I would," Jim said. "You know I'd risk my life and anything else to get you out."

"Then pretend that's me in there and try as hard as you would for me," Cat said.

"I can't do that, Cat," Jim said. "It might be you in there, if we fail. I can't risk it."

"You have no choice, Jim," Cat said. "That's what we're here for. We can't leave without them. No matter how much you hate them. We have to do what we've been trained to do."

"OK, you wait here," Jim said. "I'll see what I can do."

He was gone again for a while and when he returned, he said, "I think I've got it. I can take out the two guards outside. If I do it quietly enough, the ones inside won't know I'm there. I'll draw the attention of the other two while you run in and take these bolt cutters and see if you can cut the chains. Do you think you have enough strength to cut the chains?"

"All I can do is try," Cat answered.

"OK, let's go," Jim said, as he led Cat to the complex.

Jim caught the two outside guards, eliminated them, then carefully got into the room and fought the other two guards while Cat tried to cut the chains. They were so strong, it was hard at first, but she finally made a little headway. Jim finally eliminated the other two guards, pushed her away, grabbed the cutters and cut the chains.

"Come on, hurry. Let's get out of here," Jim said, as he pushed them toward the door.

Two more guards appeared and fired at the retreating figures. "Go, go," Jim yelled, as he stayed behind to deter the guards.

"Come on, let's go," Cat said, as she led Don and Cassidy to the drop zone.

They made it just as Greg arrived in the helicopter. "Hurry. Get on," Cat said hurrying them into the chopper, as she was constantly looking for Jim.

"Jim, where are you?" she asked.

Then she saw him running toward her with several North Koreans close behind him, firing as they went.

"Please, God," she prayed. "Let Jim get here without being shot," she said, as she turned and shot several times at Jim's pursuers. Then she climbed on board and Greg started to take off. Jim reached the chopper and Cat reached out and helped him get on board just as the chopper got airborne. The North Koreans shot, but this time, Greg was fast enough to keep from getting the chopper damaged. Cat had been holding her breath, but as soon as they were out of reach of the North Koreans' fire, she breathed a sigh of relief.

"Where are your other team members?" Jim asked, when they were finally airborne.

"The uninjured were able to get the wounded and the hostage into a chopper and get out earlier, but Cassidy and I got caught before we could make it to the chopper," Don answered. "Then they were using us as bait to lure your team down. When your team escaped without being captured, they took us back to the compound and chained us up again."

Now that everyone was safe inside the chopper, Jim said, "Let's get on back to the base, Greg."

"Sure thing, Commander Ryan. I mean, Jim," Greg answered.

Jim wrapped his arms around Cat and hugged her as hard as he could. He kissed her over and over. "I love you, Cat," he whispered into her ear. "I love you more than life itself."

"I know, Jim," Cat said. "And I love you, too."

When Cassidy and Don realized who had rescued them, Cassidy said, "Jim, I can't believe you risked your life to save me, after what I've done to you."

"You can thank Cat for that," he answered. "I wanted to just let you rot there, but she talked me into rescuing you."

"Thanks, Cat," Cassidy said. "I'm sorry that I've caused Jim and you so much trouble. I'll straighten it out when we get back home. I'm ashamed of the way I acted, now. If it had been the other way around, I don't think I would have rescued you."

"That's OK, Cassidy," Cat said. "I didn't do it for you, anyway. I did it for Jim."

"Oh," Cassidy said flatly. "Thanks, anyway."

"Yeah, thanks from me, too," Don said. "I thought we were goners. You don't know how good you both looked when I saw you come busting through that door."

"That's OK, Don," Cat said. "Some day you may return the favor."

"You bet I will, if that day ever arrives," Don answered.

"What happened to the rest of your team?" Jim asked. "Why didn't they come back and try to rescue you after they got the hostage safely back to South Korea?"

"On our original mission, most of them were injured and a couple were killed. The injured were loaded onto the chopper along with the hostage and carried to the hospital, but Cassidy and I were caught as we were trying to get to the chopper. You know the rest," Don answered.

The rest of the trip back to the base was made in silence. No one felt like making idle chit-chat. Cat could hardly wait to get back to find out how Mark and Ted were doing. She hoped their injuries weren't too serious. It looked as if their unit, as well as Don's unit, would be out of commission for a while, Jim and Cat headed to the infirmary to check on Mark and Ted as soon as they landed. They found Mark first. "Mark, how are you doing?" Jim asked.

"Well, for a guy with a bullet in his back and all these tubes stuck all over me, I guess I'm OK," he answered. "I lost a lot of blood, so they had to give me a transfusion. I think I lost consciousness a few times, so I've lost track of time. What happened to you guys?"

"We had to finish what you started," Jim answered. "Next time, don't leave such a mess. I might not be around to clean it up."

"You and Cat didn't go back over there alone did you?" Mark asked.

"No, we weren't alone," Cat answered. "God was with us the whole time."

"Did you bring them back?" Mark asked.

"Yeah, we got 'em back," Jim answered. "I didn't want to, but Cat insisted."

Just then, the nurse came in and asked them to leave. She needed to change Mark's bandage and give him a shot.

"We need to check on Ted anyway. Where can we find him?" Jim asked the nurse. She pointed them in the right direction and they found Ted with a bandage on his head and with his eyes closed.

"Ted, you OK," Jim asked, as he walked up to his bedside.

Ted didn't open his eyes or even acknowledge that they were there. Jim walked out into the hall and asked a nurse about Ted.

"Is he in a coma or something?" Jim asked.

"Are you a relative of his?" the nurse asked.

"I'm his boss," Jim said. "I need to know how he's doing."

"All I can tell you is that he had a head wound when he came into the infirmary.

He had surgery four hours ago and is being kept sedated. I'm sorry, but that's all I am allowed to tell you."

"Dang," Jim said. "I need to know if he can be moved or not. We need to get back home."

"I'm sorry, but he can't be moved right now," the nurse said. "You need to talk with his doctor for further information."

"Where are the others that came in at the same time?" Jim asked.

"One of them didn't make it. The other one is over there," she said, as she pointed to a bed on the other side of the room.

"Who didn't make it?" Cat asked, as tears filled her eyes.

"We'll have to see who's in that bed, then we'll know who didn't make it," Jim said, as he slowly led Cat over to the bed.

Fred was in the bed. Cat said a mental, "Thank you, God, it's Fred." She hated that Bill didn't make it, but at least Fred did.

"Fred, how are you doing," Jim asked, as he walked up to his bed. Fred was covered in bandages, but he held out his hand to Jim.

"Jim," he said. "I'm glad you made it. I was afraid you wouldn't come, your being suspended and all."

"Wild horses couldn't have kept me away," Jim said. "How you feeling?"

"I feel rotten, but I've felt worse," Fred said. "Is Cat all right?"

"Yes, I'm here, Fred," Cat said, as she stepped from behind Jim so that Fred could see her.

"I see you got one, too," Fred said. "Bandage, I mean. How you doing?"

"I'm OK," she answered. "I'll feel better when we get you all back home."

"Well, it looks like it'll be a while," Fred said. "Did you get the captives?"

"Yes, we did," Cat answered. "They're fine, better than you are."

The nurse came into the room to check on Fred and told them they needed to leave, so they went to find Don and Cassidy.

When they found them, Jim told them that they would have to stay in South Korea until the injured were able to be transported back to the States. "It will probably be at least three days," Jim said.

Jim, Cat, Cassidy and Don stayed at Osan AB in South Korea for three days until the injured on Jim's and Don's teams were able to be transported. Mark, Ted, Fred and the other injured were loaded into the C17 on stretchers and Bill's body, inside a flag-draped coffin, was loaded into the cargo hold of the plane.

As Jim and the others boarded the plane, he was informed that they would stop in Seattle long enough for an assessment to be made on the injured to see if they would be able to make the rest of the trip to Little Rock AFB. Bill's body would also be processed while they were there.

Jim told the others what he had learned and received a loud groan in return. "I'm sorry about the delay, but we have to think of the injured first," he said, trying to smooth it over. Then they found a place to stay on the base and wait until they could make the long flight home.

After the assessment on the injured was completed, it was determined that they would be stable enough to make it to Little Rock AFB. There, they were reassessed to see if they would need to be hospitalized there. Mark and Ted needed to be admitted to the hospital at the Little Rock AFB, but some of the others were released to continue recuperating at home.

After Jim and Cat said goodbye to Mark, Ted and Fred, they went in search of Cassidy and Don to see if they wanted a ride home. Jim had found his unit's transport van still parked where Ted had parked it days ago when they had arrived on the base to begin their long journey to South Korea. He found Don and Cassidy in the mess hall waiting for them and asked if they were ready to go home.

"You bet I'm ready," Cassidy said. "I've been here longer than I wanted to be, now. How are your team members?"

"Some bad, some better," Jim answered. "Come on let's go." Then he herded them to the van.

It was dark by the time they arrived at Don's unit headquarters. Everyone was exhausted, so they didn't take much time getting out of the vehicle.

"Thanks, again, Jim," Don said. "I'll talk to you in a few days. "Right now, I just want to go to bed."

"Yes, thanks, Jim," Cassidy said. "As soon as I can, I'll take care of those charges. Thanks, Cat. I owe you one."

Jim waited until they were inside and then he sped away. He could hardly wait to get home and into bed, also.

He hoped that Cassidy would be true to her word and that she would get him cleared of those charges. Then he could get his life back. He wondered if there would be repercussions from this mission; he was still on suspension. Would the Review Board take into consideration the reason he disobeyed their order. Surely one of them had a wife that he loved. Surely he would understand why he had to go rescue Cat. If they didn't understand, he was in really bad trouble. He thought maybe he could live with that, but he knew he couldn't live without Cat. "I guess that would be a fair trade," he thought. He didn't like it, but he would accept it as long as he had Cat.

CHAPTER 12

On the following Monday, Jim was called to appear before the Review Board again. He really dreaded what they would say this time. He was expecting to be dismissed because of insubordination. Still he and Cat showed up at the Boardroom at his appointed time.

"Commander Ryan, will you come in and shut the door," the Commissioner asked. When Jim was in the room, the Commissioner told him to be seated.

"First, I want to tell you that Agent Love has dropped all the charges against you."

"Thank you, Sir," Jim said, as he breathed a sigh of relief. At least Cassidy kept her word.

"Next, I have a problem with you that I haven't decided how to handle," the Commissioner said. "You were commanded to have nothing to do with the execution of the North Korean rescue operation assigned to your unit while you were suspended, were you not?"

"Yes, Sir, I was," Jim answered.

"Then how is it that you were able to rescue your team and Commander Gardner's team using a Commission helicopter and pilot?" the Commissioner asked.

"They needed me and there was no one else to go," Jim answered.

"Could you not have notified your superior and let him handle it?" the Commissioner asked.

"There was no time. I had to do what I did or they would have been captured, maybe even tortured. I couldn't let that happen," Jim answered.

"Because your wife was one of them, I suppose," the Commissioner asked sarcastically.

"Yes, Sir, because my wife was one of them," Jim answered.

"Commander Ryan, you have been called before the Board four times now and all four times, your wife has been involved in your disobedience. Isn't that correct?" the Commissioner asked.

"Not exactly, Sir, if you mean that because of her, I have disobeyed the rules," Jim stated.

"How would you put it, then?" the Commissioner asked.

"Yes, Sir, I did what I did to protect my wife, but I would have done the same thing to protect any of my team members," Jim answered.

"That's what you say, but I doubt that you would have done the same thing, if it had been someone else," the Commissioner said sarcastically.

"Sir, what are you getting at?" Jim asked.

"I just think that you're too focused on your wife to do your job properly," the Commissioner said.

"Sir, are you married?" Jim asked.

"No, I'm divorced," the Commissioner said. "What does that have to do with this?"

"When you were first married, did you love your wife?" Jim asked.

"Yes, of course, if I hadn't loved her, I wouldn't have married her," he answered.

"Sir, my wife and I have only been married one year," Jim stated. "Maybe after we've been married longer, I won't be so focused on her, as you call it, but right now, she is almost my whole world. I couldn't stand it if anything happened to her. I'll do my job as long as it doesn't interfere with the safety of my wife. When it does, I'll take steps to keep her safe. No matter what that entails."

"I guess you've made that clear enough, Commander Ryan," the

Commissioner said. "In other words, you'll obey the rules, until your wife is in danger, then you'll disobey them. Is that correct?"

"Not exactly, Sir," Jim answered, getting angry "I just mean that I will do whatever it takes to keep my wife safe. If that means giving up the job I have had most of my life and that I dearly love, so be it."

"Do you have anything else to say concerning your recent actions?" the Commissioner asked.

"No, Sir," Jim answered.

"Then, will you step out into the waiting room while we make our decision?" the Commissioner said.

Jim stood and walked slowly toward the door. He didn't have a good feeling about their decision, but at least he got to tell them how he felt. That was more than he had expected when he walked into the room.

"How did it go?" Cat asked, as he walked over to her and kissed her.

"I don't know," Jim answered. "They're trying to give me a hard time. It went better than I had expected, though. Cassidy dropped the charges. That's one thing in my favor, but I still have the insubordination charge to face."

"We'll get through it, Jim," Cat said, as she rubbed his back. "No matter what the outcome is, we'll get through it."

"I know we will, Cat," Jim said. "As long as I still have you, I think I can face anything."

After about an hour, Jim was called back into the Boardroom.

"Be seated, Commander Ryan," the Commissioner began. "It is the decision of the Board to reinstate you to your former position as Commander of your unit."

Jim almost fainted from relief. He said a mental, "Thank you, God."

"Since Agent Love admitted that the charges she made against you were false, then you should never have been on suspension," the Commissioner continued. "If you had not been on suspension, then you would have been with your unit. Since you were not with your unit when they were in trouble, you had every right to act as you did to rescue them. Therefore, there should have been no insubordination charges made against you. That is the ruling of this Board of Review. We do not want to see you brought before this Review Board again. Please refrain from trying to kill people who touch your wife. Do you think you can do that?" the Commissioner asked.

"I'll try, Sir. Thank you and the whole Board. I'll really try to stay out of trouble," Jim happily replied.

"Now, will you send in your wife? We would like to talk to her alone for a few minutes," the Commissioner asked.

"Please be seated, Agent Ryan," the Commissioner said to Cat, as he indicated a seat in front of the members of the Board.

"You've been here before, I believe. Is that right Agent Ryan?" the Commissioner asked.

"Yes, Sir," Cat answered.

"You may be wondering why I asked you to come here today," he said.

"Yes, Sir," Cat answered.

"Commander Ryan seems to be unusually focused on your safety. That seems to be a problem of his. He was an exceptional Commander before his marriage. Now, he is putting your safety before his assignment from the Commission. This has caused him to be called before the Review Board several times. I wonder if there may be something that you can do to prevent any future reprimands to Commander Ryan?" the Commissioner asked.

"What do you mean, Sir?" Cat asked.

"I mean that you seem to be going out of your way to cause trouble for Commander Ryan," the Commissioner said. "If that is the case, I request that you stop and consider what you're doing to his brilliant career."

"Sir, I have not intentionally done anything to hamper Commander Ryan's career," Cat answered angrily. "What Jim did, he did to protect me, his wife. He did what any normal, sane man, who loved his wife, would do," Cat continued. "I don't know what you expect me to do, but I'm going to continue to be Jim Ryan's wife and I'm sure that he will continue to want to protect me. I'm proud that he wants to protect me and I'm proud to be working with him in a dangerous job. I've been trained to be able to protect him in return and I will do that to the best of my ability. Now, I don't know what else you wanted me to say," Cat finished, with a tilt of her head to show her defiance.

"I think you just answered my question, Agent Ryan," the Commissioner said. "I don't think Commander Ryan will have to be as focused on your protection as he once was. I think you two will make a great team. I just hope I never see Commander Ryan called before the Review Board again. You may go. Please tell Commander Ryan to come back in for a few minutes on your way out."

"They want to see you again, Jim," Cat said, as she entered the waiting area.

"Commander Ryan," the Commissioner said. "Your wife seems to be capable of protecting herself now. You shouldn't have to be so focused on her protection. She proved herself capable during the training competition. Therefore, we shouldn't have to see you again because you were protecting your wife. Do I make myself clear, Commander Ryan?"

"Yes, Sir," Jim answered.

"Then you are dismissed. I don't want to see you again," the Commissioner stated.

"I don't want to see you again either, Sir," Jim said and he turned and walked out of the room.

"What did they say?" Cat asked.

"They said they didn't want to see me again," Jim said happily. "I said that suits the heck out of me. Come on. Let's go home."

It seemed strange to Jim, coming home and finding none of his team there. Either Mark or Ted was always there except when they were out on an assignment. Tomorrow, he would have to see about arrangements for Bill's body to be transported to his hometown

151

for burial. He didn't know if Bill had family or not, but he would find that out in the morning. Right now, he was exhausted. He just wanted to go to bed and forget the bad things that had happened. Would he ever be able to forget them, though. With Cat's help, maybe he could forget some of them. He put his arm around her shoulders and said," Come to bed, Hon. We have a tough day ahead of us tomorrow."

So they went up the stairs and into their bedroom, but they didn't go to sleep right away. They had some making up to do, and they did.

CHAPTER 13

Jim drove from home to meet the airplane that brought Bill Lawrence's body from the mortuary in Seattle into the Lackland AFB. When Jim arrived at the air base, he was met by Bill's parents, Mr. and Mrs. Harvey Lawrence. Bill was only 23 years old. He had been a member of Jim's team for only two years, but Jim had come to like him very much. Jim was very sad to have to bring Bill's body home to his grieving parents.

"Mr. and Mrs. Lawrence, I'm Jim Ryan. I was Bill's Commander. I'm so sorry for your loss. He was a fine agent. He will really be missed by my unit."

"Thank you, Commander Ryan. We appreciate your kind words," Mrs. Lawrence said, as she wiped away her tears. "Bill really thought a lot of you. He was so proud to be a member of your unit. He talked about you all the time. He loved being an FSC Agent. We thank you for bringing him home."

"If there is anything I can do for you, Mrs. Lawrence, please let me know," Jim said, as he took her hands into his and gave them a squeeze. "I know there's nothing that can compensate you for the loss of your precious son, but just let me know if there's anything I can do to help."

"Will you attend his funeral?" Mrs. Lawrence asked.

"Yes, Ma'am, I'll be there," Jim answered. "I'll stay a few days afterward to help tie up any loose ends, if you need me. Here's my cell phone number. Just call me if you need me."

"Will you go to the funeral home to make the arrangements with us?" Mrs. Lawrence asked.

"Yes, Ma'am, of course," Jim answered.

"Would you like to come stay with us while you're here?" Mrs. Lawrence asked.

"No, thank you, Mrs. Lawrence," Jim answered. "I have already made arrangements to stay here on base. I appreciate the offer, anyway. I'm sure my wife appreciates it, also. She always worries that I don't eat right or get enough rest."

"I know how wives are," Mrs. Lawrence said. "I'm one, too."

"Yes, she is," Mr. Lawrence agreed. "We would love to have you stay with us, but I know you need to be here to take care of business. Thanks, again, for taking such good care of our son. Like my wife said, he thought a lot of you. He wanted to be like you some day. I guess he'll never get that chance now," Mr. Lawrence said, then he took his handkerchief out of his pocket and wiped the tears from his eyes.

"Here's the funeral car, now," Jim said, as a hearse backed up to the plane and the attendants jumped out and prepared to load Bill's body into the back.

"I'll ride in the car with Bill to the funeral home," Jim said. "I'll meet you two there. Do you know what funeral home?"

"Yes," Mr. Lawrence said. "We'll see you there."

At the funeral home, Jim sat with the grieving parents while they made the arrangements. The funeral was set for Wednesday at 2:00 p.m. That would be two days until Bill's funeral. Jim had to take care of the business of closing Bill's file and some other business that needed his attention, anyway, so he was glad that he would have time to do it before he had to return home.

Bill's father drove Jim back to the base where he had left his car and ridden in the funeral car with Bill's body. Jim wanted to get settled before calling Cat. He was anxious to hear her voice, but he wanted to have plenty of time to talk to her. He thanked Mr.

Lawrence and said that he would see him later. Then he went to the room on the base where he would stay while he was there.

When he was settled in his room, he made his call. "Hi, Hon," he said, when she answered his call. "I made it. Everything went as planned. I would have called sooner, but Bill's parents wanted me to accompany them to the funeral home when they made the arrangements. I'm back on the base now."

"I was getting anxious," Cat said. "I could hardly wait to hear from you. I miss you already."

"I miss you, too," Jim said. "I'll have to be here a few days, though. There are some things I have to do before the funeral and the funeral won't be until Wednesday. How are things going?"

"I talked to Mark this morning," Cat said. "He said he may be coming home tomorrow. I thought I would take care of him like I did before, if that's OK with you."

"Sure, as long as he doesn't try to steal you, like he did last time," Jim said.

"No chance of that," Cat said. Then she gave a little laugh. She thought Jim was just kidding. "Mark said that Ted is doing better. They've been getting him up a little at a time. It'll probably be a few more days, though, before he can come home."

"I have to go now, Hon, they're calling me," Jim said quickly. "You take care of things while I'm gone. Be safe. I love you. Gotta go now. Bye."

"I love you, Jim," Cat said, as Jim ended the call. She suddenly felt empty. She would have liked to have ended the call differently, but she knew that when Jim said he had to go, he had to go quickly. She sure was going to miss him. Maybe he would call again soon. She had to talk to him again before bedtime. She wouldn't be able to sleep unless she did.

Jim called again about bedtime. "Hi, Hon," he said. "I just wanted to hear your voice again before you went to bed. How are things going?"

"Just about the same," she answered. She was so happy to hear his voice again before she went to bed. "Mark called again. He said they would be releasing him on Wednesday. I'm going to drive to the hospital and pick him up. He has no other way to get home. He didn't want to come in an ambulance, since he's getting better."

"Well, you just be careful," Jim worried. "I don't like the idea of your going that far alone. Is there anyone who can go with you?"

"I won't be alone, Jim," Cat said. "God will be with me. It's not that far, anyway."

"I know how far it is," Jim said. "I just drove it the other night, and it's far. Please be careful. Don't let any strangers get in the car with you."

"Yes, Daddy," Cat said sarcastically. "I'll be real careful. Of course I won't let any strangers ride with me. I'll be all right, Jim. You just take care of yourself. I love you and miss you so much, Jim," she said. "Please hurry home."

"I'll start home as soon as the funeral is over. I'll call again tomorrow. Gotta go now. Love you. Bye."

Then he was gone. It's funny how empty the house felt without him. He was so much a part of her that it seemed as if half of her was missing when he wasn't there.

She got dressed for bed and snuggled down under the covers. "The sooner I go to sleep the sooner it'll be morning and I can talk to him again," she thought. She drifted off to sleep, dreaming of a white knight on a beautiful white stallion coming to rescue her from the fire-breathing dragon.

The next morning, Cat hurriedly dressed and ran downstairs for breakfast. Barbara was already in the kitchen preparing breakfast. She already had coffee brewing and the smell was very inviting.

"Good morning, Barbara," Cat said cheerfully.

"Good morning, Cat," Barbara replied. "You sound awfully happy this morning. Will Jim be home today?"

"Not today, but maybe tomorrow," Cat answered. "The funeral is tomorrow at 2:00 p.m. Jim said he would leave as soon as it was over. It'll probably be late tomorrow, but maybe he'll be home tomorrow night. Oh, and I'm going to the hospital to pick up Mark tomorrow, so I'll be gone, too. There'll probably be no one here for you to prepare meals for until we all get back."

"That'll be unusual," Barbara said. "I guess I'll just take a day off, then."

"Sure, you can do anything you want to do. It'll be just like a holiday for you," Cat said.

"No, not like a holiday, because I'm usually very busy on holidays. It'll be a rest day," Barbara said.

Cat's phone rang and she grabbed it. It was Jim. "Hi, Hon," he said. "How are you doing?"

"I'm fine, how about you?" she asked.

"Missing you," he said. "I plan to spend the day with Mr. and Mrs. Lawrence.

They've been bugging me to come for a visit. I just feel like I need to spend some time with them before I come home tomorrow. If I can get away from here by 4:00 p.m. tomorrow afternoon, I should be home by Midnight, or 1:00 a.m. at least. Do you still plan to go pick up Mark tomorrow?"

"Yes, I do," Cat answered.

"Well, you be really careful," he said.

"You be careful, too. You'll be driving late. Be sure and don't fall asleep at the wheel. If you get sleepy, stop and take a nap," Cat said.

"I'm used to driving late at night, Cat," he answered. "You just make sure you drive safely. I don't want to lose you."

When he ended the call, Cat felt the same emptiness that she had felt each time he ended his call before. She would be so glad when he was home again. This day would probably just drag by, so she would have to find something to do to make it go faster.

She decided to go upstairs and get Mark's room ready for his arrival. She changed the sheets and vacuumed and dusted the room. As she was dusting the dresser, she picked up a notebook in which Mark kept notes. As she picked it up, something fell out of it. It was a sheet of paper folded into a square. Cat curiously unfolded it. It was a sketch that Mark had made of her. It was a side view and it looked like she was busy doing something. She could tell by the look on her face that she was deeply concentrating on whatever she was doing. It was such a good likeness that she caught her breath at the minute details that he had put into it. At the bottom, he had written, "The Beautiful Cat, the Woman I love."

"Oh, no, this can't be," Cat thought. "Surely it doesn't mean what I think it means. What was that that Jim had said? 'As long as he doesn't try to steal you.' I didn't pay any attention to that. I just thought that Jim was just teasing me."

She tried to think back to the time before when Mark had been injured. What had he said? What did he say when he asked her to put her hand on his forehead? He said he needed some TLC. She told him to call Jenny. He did, but she left in a huff. Jim was so angry with Mark that time. "I couldn't understand why he was so angry. Did it have something to do with how Mark felt about me?" she wondered.

She folded the picture and put it back on the dresser where it had been. She walked slowly out of the room. "This can't be what it looks like," she thought. "If it is, how will I be able to face Mark?"

She really had no way of knowing who the artist was, since there was no signature. Mark had never done anything to suggest that he was in love with her. She always thought of him as a big brother and she felt that he thought of her as a younger sister. Jim was always asking Mark to take care of her and protect her when he had to be away.

Now, she wondered if that was the reason Jim had been so angry when Mark had told her he needed some TLC. "What was that that Jim had said when I told him I was going to get Mark and bring him home? It was something about trying to steal me like he did the last time. I thought Jim was just trying to be funny, but maybe he was serious." I have to get these thoughts out of my head, or I won't be able to face Mark," Cat thought. "Then, that long ride home. I can't go, thinking he's in love with me. There has to be some other reason for those words on a picture of me. There just has to be. He can't be in love with me. He just can't."

By the time Jim called her that night, Cat had gotten herself so worked up that she had a bad tension headache. She knew she couldn't say anything to Jim. If she did, he would get angry again and probably tell her she couldn't go get Mark. Jim must know how Mark felt about her or he wouldn't have said what he did.

"Hi, Hon," Jim said, as usual when he called.

"Hi, yourself, Jim," Cat said. She knew she couldn't let Jim know how upset she was.

"How you doing tonight, Hon?" Jim asked.

"I have a slight headache," Cat said. "It's nothing, though. It'll go away soon. I took some aspirin."

"Are you sure you're OK?" Jim asked. He sounded worried, so Cat had to reassure him that she was fine.

"I can't wait to get home to you," he said. "Have there been any problems that you couldn't handle?" he asked.

She thought "Yes, there is one," but she said, "No, I can handle anything now, Jim. Everything is going as smoothly as clockwork."

"Well, I guess I'll see you sometime around Midnight tomorrow, if all goes well," he said. "Now you be really careful when you go pick up Mark. I wish you'd take someone with you. Is Carol home? Maybe she'd go if she's home."

"No, Carol and Skip won't be home until April or May," she answered. "I'll be all right, Jim. Don't worry about me. Just worry about yourself and get home safely."

"I wish Carol was at home," Cat thought. "It might be better to have someone with me when I face Mark." At least Mark didn't know that she had found the drawing.

That was one thing in her favor. Now, if she could just force herself to stop thinking about it and go to sleep, maybe she could make it tomorrow.

The next morning, she was up early. She dressed and hurried

downstairs to breakfast. Barbara had already prepared a delicious meal for her.

"I knew you would want to get an early start, so I fixed it as soon as I could," Barbara said.

"Thanks, Barbara," Cat said as she filled her plate and prepared to eat. "I don't know when Mark and I will be back, so I'll call you when I get close to home to let you know approximately when we'll arrive. Jim said he probably wouldn't be home until about Midnight, so you don't have to worry about him."

"Thanks, Cat. I appreciate your letting me know," Barbara said.

As soon as Cat finished eating, she grabbed a pillow, some blankets and a first-aid kit and headed for her car. She still didn't know how bad Mark's wounds were, so she wanted to be prepared for anything. After she loaded the car, she told Barbara goodbye and headed for the hospital where Mark, Ted and the others were recuperating.

It was a long trip, but she finally arrived. She hurried out of the car and down to Mark's room. When she walked into his room, she found Mark lying on the bed fully clothed except for his shoes, watching the TV.

"Hi, Cat," Mark said when he saw her.

"Hi, Mark, are you ready to go?" she asked.

"Yes, I just have to sign some papers and get a prescription and some instructions from the nurse. She told me to call her when you got here," Mark said as he pushed the off button on the TV remote control, then he pushed the call button and the nurse asked if she could help him.

"My ride is here," he answered.

"I'll be down in a few minutes," she answered.

In a few minutes, the nurse arrived with the papers for Mark to sign and the other things. Then she gave him a pain shot. She said maybe that would make the long trip more comfortable for him. She brought a wheelchair and had him get into it and then pushed him out to Cat's car and helped him get into the car.

"I brought a pillow and some blankets, if you want to lie down in back," Cat said.

"No, I think I'll just sit up front with you," he answered, as the nurse helped him into the front passenger seat. Then she fastened his seat belt and closed the door. It wasn't long before Mark leaned back, closed his eyes and was asleep. The shot was working.

After driving for an hour, Cat had to stop for a rest. As soon as the car stopped moving, Mark woke up.

"Are we home already?" he asked.

"No, I just had to take a break," Cat answered.

"Do you want to get out?" she asked.

"Yes, I do," Mark said, as he struggled to get out. "Can you help me?"

"Put your arm around my shoulders and I'll support you until we get to the door," she said, as she helped him out.

She stopped at the men's restroom door and said, "You'll have to go the rest of the way on your own."

"Thanks, Cat," he said. "Will you help me back to the car?"

"Yes, I'll help you," she said and she went on to the ladies restroom.

When Cat came back by, Mark was waiting for her. He put his arm around her shoulders, as before, and she helped him to the car.

"I'll go get us something to drink and a snack," she said. She was back in a few minutes and started on the road again. It wasn't long before Mark was asleep again.

"Good," Cat thought. "As long as he's asleep, he isn't in pain."

When she finally arrived at the cabin, it was just about 3:00 p.m. She helped Mark into the cabin and over to the sofa in the den.

"I'm glad you made it back OK," Barbara said. "I have some sandwiches made for you. Are you hungry?"

"I am," Mark said. "My snack didn't last very long."

Barbara brought the sandwiches and some Cokes into the den and after a short blessing, they hungrily ate the sandwiches.

About 10:00 p.m., Cat said, "I'm so tired, I think I'll go on upstairs to bed. Do you need anything else, Mark?"

"Would you mind changing my bandage?" he asked. "I can't reach it very well. It feels like it needs changing."

"Sure," Cat said. She got the bandages and other things with which to change it and had Mark pull his shirt off.

The memory of the drawing of her and the words at the bottom flashed through her mind, as she looked at his strong, muscular back. She tried to push the thought out of her mind and concentrate on what she was doing. It was good that Mark had slept all the way home, because then she wasn't forced to face him, but this was different. When she touched his body, she felt him jerk and she pulled her hand away quickly. "I can't do this," she thought. "I have to, though. He can't do it by himself." So she clenched her teeth and rewrapped Mark's wound as quickly as she could.

"Cat," Mark said when she finished. "Thank you. I guess it must have been hard for you, but I appreciate it. When Jim gets here, I'll ask him to do it next time."

"That's OK, Mark," Cat said, as she looked away from Mark and headed toward the stairs. "I can do it. I'm just so tired. I'll see you in the morning." Then she ran up the stairs as quickly as she could. It wasn't good for her to be alone with Mark for very long.

Cat was so tired that she was asleep almost as soon as her head touched the pillow. About Midnight, Jim finally arrived home. He turned the lamp on in the hallway to see where he was going.

"Is that you, Jim?" Mark asked, raising up to see.

"Yes, it's me," Jim answered, as he walked over to the sofa. "How are you feeling?"

"Tired," Mark answered. "It was a long, hard trip. I guess you had a long, hard one, too."

"Yeah, I did," Jim said, as he sat down in a recliner and looked at Mark.

"Mark, I want you to remember what I told you the last time

Cat took care of you," Jim said. "That still goes. I just want you to know where I stand."

"I remember, Jim," Mark said. "I'll keep my thoughts and my hands to myself.

It's hard, but I don't want any trouble with you."

"Let's just keep it that way," Jim said. "As long as we have an understanding, we'll get along just fine. Is there anything you need before I go upstairs?" Jim asked, as he rose from the chair.

"No, I don't need anything that you can give me," Mark said.

Jim frowned, shook his head and walked on up the stairs.

Cat had been asleep, but had awakened when she heard Jim's car pull into the driveway. She had turned on the bedside lamp and had expected Jim to come on up. She was wondering what was taking so long. She went to the door and she could hear Jim and Mark talking. She couldn't tell what they were saying, but it didn't sound like friendly chatter. When she heard Jim start up the stairs, she jumped back into bed. As Jim opened the bedroom door, he said, "Hi, Hon, did I wake you up?"

"I was already awake," she said.

She jumped out of bed and kissed him and gave him a big hug. "I'm so glad you're finally home safe and sound," she said.

"I told you it would be about Midnight," he said.

"I know, but it seemed like an eternity," Cat answered. "Did you have any trouble?"

"No, I didn't. Did you?" he asked.

"Not any, surprisingly," she said. "Mark slept almost all the way home, so he wasn't in a lot of pain. That helped my nerves. I would have been tense, if I had thought he had been in pain."

"Yeah, I guess so," Jim frowned and started to undress. "Did you find out anything else about Ted and the others?" he asked.

"They should be ready to come home in a couple more days," she answered.

Cat got back into bed and waited for Jim to lie down. As he got into the bed, he pulled her to him and said, "I sure missed my bed partner," and he began to kiss her passionately. They made love and then Jim turned over and went to sleep. Cat looked at her sleeping husband and her heart filled up with love for him. How had she ever been so lucky to have gotten such a wonderful husband. She knew she would have to be very careful around Mark. She knew how jealous Jim was of her and she didn't want to cause any trouble between her and Jim. She liked Mark a lot, but if she ever had to choose between the two of them, it would definitely be Jim who would win hands down. She lay there for a while watching her sleeping husband and thanked God for him. Finally she drifted off to sleep.

The next morning, after breakfast, Jim asked Cat to come into his office. He handed Mark his crutches and told him to come in, also.

"We're far from being a full unit," Jim began, but we can still do some recon.

Mark, how long before you feel like trying to get out and do something?"

"I don't know," Mark answered. "Maybe a few days. Let me get off this pain medicine first or I'll go to sleep on you."

"OK, Cat, you and I can do a recon nearby until Mark is ready," Jim said. We've gotten a tip about a group of terrorists over on the east side of town. You and I will go scout it out tonight."

"Are you sure you want to take Cat out without any backup?" Mark asked.

"Yes, she can handle it," Jim said angrily. "Can't you, Cat?"

"Of course, I can," she answered.

"That's settled then," Jim said. "I'll finish making our plans. You can go back to what you were doing, Cat. Mark, I'd like to talk to you alone, if you don't mind. Cat, would you close the door when you go out?"

Cat left and closed the door behind her. When she was gone, Jim looked at Mark and angrily said, "Mark, don't try to come between Cat and me. When I tell Cat to do something, I expect her to obey my command. I don't need you to tell her that I'm making a mistake. I told you not to try to cause trouble between my wife and me. I thought you said you understood."

"I do understand, Jim, but there's no reason to put Cat in danger just to make a point," Mark said.

"She won't be in danger," Jim said angrily. "She's a good agent. You should have seen her in the training class. She's smart, too. She might even be one of the best agents I have. You just tend to your own business and let me take care of mine. If you don't like what I'm doing, you can always transfer to another unit. In light of the fact that you're in love with my wife, that might be the best thing for all of us."

"Jim, you don't mean what you're saying," Mark said. "We've been together for 10 years. I don't want to work with anyone else."

"Then stay out of my business and leave my wife alone," Jim said.

"Jim, I'm sorry," Mark said. "I apologize. I'm sorry for being in love with your wife. I can't help that, but I told you that I would never try to take her away from you and I won't. I know I couldn't, anyway. Also, I will stay out of your business. Just let me continue to work with you and Cat. If I can't have her, at least let me be close to her."

"I'll work with you, if you keep your promise, but the first time I see you trying anything with Cat, you're gone. Now, do I make myself clear this time? That's the deal. Take it or leave it. Leave my wife alone."

"Sure, Jim, I heard you loud and clear. I'll look, but I won't touch. Do you think we can work together, since you have so much animosity toward me?" Mark asked.

"I don't have animosity toward you, Mark," Jim said. "I just want you to know where your boundaries are and I want you to respect them. If you do that, then I think we can still work together. You step over that line one time, and you're gone. Now, if there's nothing else you want to say to me, you may go. I have work to do."

"That's all I have to say, Jim," Mark said. Then he went out the door with the aid of his crutches and shut the door behind him. All of a sudden, he was drained of all of his energy. He made it to the sofa, fell down and lay back on his pillow. "Why did I have to pick Jim's wife to fall in love with?" Mark asked himself. "Of all the women in the world, I had to fall in love with Cat."

That night, Jim and Cat set up a surveillance at the terrorists' house. They recorded their comings and goings. They took notes of what was brought into the house and what was taken out of it.

When they came back to the cabin about 2:00 a.m., Mark was asleep, but as they turned on the hall lamp, he awoke.

"How did it go?" Mark asked sleepily.

"It was about what I expected," Jim answered. "They're getting ready to blow something up all right. We just have to tap into their line to find out what."

"Come on, Cat," Jim said, as he headed up the stairs. "Let's go to bed."

"Is there anything you need before I go to bed?" Cat asked Mark.

"My bandage needs to be changed again. Would you mind doing that, again?" Mark asked.

"Sure, where are the bandages?" Cat asked.

"Here, I tried to do it myself, but I just can't reach it."

"Cat, are you coming?" Jim called from the top of the stairs.

"In a minute, Jim," Cat answered. "I just need to bandage Mark's wound."

Jim was angry, but he knew that Mark couldn't bandage his wound himself. He decided to make it a point to do it himself the next time. He didn't like Cat getting that close to Mark. He had already threatened Mark. If he tried anything with Cat, he would carry through on his threat. He stood at the top of the stairs and watched. Then he felt ashamed of himself. He trusted Cat, even if he didn't trust Mark. He knew Cat wouldn't do anything to endanger their marriage. She loved him and he loved her and he would just have to trust that she would never betray that trust. So he just turned and walked on into the bedroom and undressed.

This time when Mark pulled his shirt off and Cat touched his back, there wasn't the same reaction as there had been the first time. Maybe he was getting used to her touch and she was getting used to touching him. Whatever it was, Cat was glad that that same spark wasn't there this time.

She hurriedly dressed his wound and Mark replaced his shirt. "Thanks, Cat. I appreciate it. Maybe it won't be too much longer before it's healed and won't need to be bandaged again."

"It looks like it's healing nicely," Cat said. "Well, is there anything else?"

"No, that's all," Mark answered.

"Good night, then," Cat said. "I'll see you in the morning."

"Good night, Cat, sweet dreams," Mark said. "I'll probably have some," he thought as he watched Cat run up the stairs and into their bedroom.

Mark sighed and lay down and tried to go back to sleep. This was going to be more difficult than he had thought. Maybe he should consider transferring. No, maybe he could stand it. He liked working with Jim and he loved being close to Cat. He'd have to decide which would be the hardest, being close to Cat and unable to do anything about it or not seeing her at all. He thought not seeing her at all would probably be the worse thing. He would just have to wait and see. He noticed that Jim had stood and watched him for a few minutes and then he had gone on into the bedroom Maybe he was beginning to trust him again. He would just have to try and earn Jim's trust again. Soon he was asleep, and the morning sun was beginning to peep through the window.

CHAPTER 14

The next night, Jim and Cat went again to the terrorists' building. "Cat, cover me. I have to get closer and see if I can figure out what they intend to blow up?" Jim said.

Jim made his way to the phone terminal and put a tap on it. Then he inched his way up as close as he could get to the window. He could see four men working on something that looked like a bomb. The four men were speaking in a language with which Jim was unfamiliar, so he recorded what he could. He figured he would send the recording to the decoding department and maybe they could make out what the men were saying.

One of them must have seen Jim, because he said something and pointed to where Jim was hidden. Jim hurried back to the vehicle and yelled, "Go, Cat, go," as he jumped into the vehicle. The men started shooting, as Jim finally got the door closed and returned their fire.

Cat drove as fast as she could and turned at random corners to confuse the men in case they followed them. When they were sure that they had lost the terrorists, Jim said, "OK, Cat. Let's go home."

The next morning, Jim took the tapes to the FSC headquarters to give to the decoding department. After a few days, they found that the terrorists intended to bomb the Federal Training Academy, that was now in its new building in Jonesboro. The Academy would hold a graduation ceremony on May 20. There would be hundreds of visitors, as well as a hundred graduates.

Jim knew that he would have to round up the terrorists before that day. Mark was still in no shape to help, so Jim started riding him to get well faster. Mark, of course, felt that Jim was doing it because of their conflict about Cat.

"Mark, you need to try harder," Jim said one day when Mark had given up doing his exercises because of the pain.

"Leave me alone, Jim," Mark shouted. "You don't know how I feel. I can stand only so much pain."

"You can stand more than you think, Mark," Jim said. "Get back to work doing your exercises. You need to do 10 more reps before you quit."

"Jim, when I get better, I'm going to pound you into the ground," Mark threatened.

"You have to get better first," Jim said.

While Mark was exercising and trying to get stronger, Jim was interviewing applicants for a replacement for Bill. Ted and Fred had come home from the hospital, but were still unable to go on assignment. None of the applicants met with Jim's expectations, so his team was still short.

Finally, Mark was ready to get back to work, but that still made only Jim, Cat and Mark on Jim's team.

One day, Don Gardner called and asked Jim if he and his team could help him on an assignment. He said that his team had been ordered to rescue another hostage from the North Koreans because they were familiar with the area. They had rescued the hostage, but in so doing, three of Don's team members had been captured and were being held in North Korea. "I'm short a few men, Don. I just have Mark and Cat."

"Well, you three and Cassidy and me make five. Don't you think the five of us can handle it?"

"Maybe. If you know where they're being held and we don't have to run all over the darn country looking for them," Jim answered.

"I have them spotted on the computer," Don answered. "We can't go in like we've been doing, though. They're on to us now. We have to go in the back way, over the mountains. It'll be rough, but that's the only way we can do it."

"Send me the information and let me study it," Jim answered.

"Its on it's way," Don answered, as he sent the information to Jim's computer.

Jim studied the information for a while and then he called Mark and Cat into his office. "Here's the plan," Jim began. "The chopper will drop us here. Then we go over the mountain here," Jim said as he pointed to an area on the screen. "We'll come up behind the compound, free the men and get back out the same way."

"That looks rough," Mark answered. "That's two trips over the mountain. You know they'll be after us the whole time. We won't be able to go very fast."

"So what do you think, then?" Jim asked. "Can we make it?"

"It'll be rough, Jim," Mark answered. "Are you sure you want to take Cat?"

"I can go anywhere you can go, Mark Fuller," Cat said angrily. "You just try to keep me from going."

"Well, there you have it, Mark," Jim said. "Cat wants to go, so let's give it a try."

"I really don't like it, Jim," Mark said. "I'll go, though, so I can protect Cat."

Jim frowned at Mark's last sentence. Jim knew that he would never deliberately put Cat in danger. He also knew that they couldn't carry out the assignment without her. He would just have to be especially careful to make sure she was safe.

The plan worked well at first, but after they freed Don's team members, they somehow got separated from Don and his team. When they got to the mountain pass where they were supposed to cross, there was no sign of Don and his team. They had apparently been picked up by another chopper.

As they reached the mountain pass that they had come over by, Jim felt that something was wrong. "You wait here, Cat," Jim said. "Mark and I'll go up and check out this pass."

Halfway up the mountain, the pass was blocked by a rock slide that had occurred after they had used it when they first came over the mountain. To get around the rock slide, Jim and Mark had to inch their way along a one-inch wide ledge. Jim decided to go first to see if it could be done. He stepped on some loose rocks and before he could catch himself, he was over the cliff. He grabbed at the side of the rock on the way down and cut his hands. As he hung there bleeding, he looked down. He was hundreds of feet from the ground, so the only way out was up.

"Mark, help me," Jim called.

Mark hurried to the edge and looked down at Jim. A quick thought flashed through his mind. This was the answer to his problems. If Jim fell, Cat would be a widow and he would be able to win her love. Jim's position as Commander would be open and, since he was Jim's Second-in-Command, he would naturally be promoted to it.

"Mark, grab my hand. I'm slipping," Jim shouted. "I can't hold on much longer."

Mark hesitated for only a second. He could never live with himself if he let Jim die. Every time he looked into Cat's eyes he would see Jim's face. Mark lay down on the rock and leaned over as far as he could. He extended both hands to Jim.

"Grab my hands, Jim," he said, as he gripped Jim's hands as tightly as he could and pulled with all of his might.

When Jim was safe, they both lay on the rocks and caught their breaths. Jim looked at Mark with a stern face, "You thought about it didn't you, Mark?" he asked. "If I had been in your position, I don't know if I would have done it the way you did. Thanks, anyway. I appreciate your saving my life."

Mark just shrugged his shoulders and silently walked back down to where they had left Cat.

"How did it go?" Cat asked anxiously.

"Not too good," Jim answered. "We can't go that way. We have to go around."

"But won't that take longer?" Cat asked.

"Yes, it will, but we have no other choice," Jim said. "Come on, let's go. The sun's going down. It'll be dark soon and it gets awfully cold here after dark."

They hurried along as fast as they could. Cat's legs felt like she was walking in wet cement. "I'm so tired. Can't we stop for a few minutes?" she asked.

"No, we have to keep moving," Jim answered. "We have to get as close to the border and our pickup point as we can before it's too dark. I'm sure the North Koreans are pretty close behind us. We used a lot of time having to backtrack."

Finally it was too dark to see where they were going. Jim picked out a nice sheltered area enclosed by rocks on each side. "We'll stop here until it gets light again," he said. "Our pilot will probably guess that we had to stay here until morning. I hope he has already picked up Don and his team. I'm sorry, Cat, we can't have a fire. We would be giving away our position. We'll just have to cuddle."

Cat snuggled up as close to Jim as she could and he hugged her to his chest as tightly as he could. "I like to cuddle," she said. "Mark, do you want to cuddle with us?"

"No, Cat, I'm OK," he said, as he sat down opposite them and watched. He wished he could cuddle with Cat, but he knew Jim would be very angry with him if he did, so he just wrapped his arms around himself and tried to stay warm.

As soon as it was light, Jim got them up and going again. "Oh," Cat said as she tried to stand. "I'm so stiff."

"Come on, Cat. We have to get moving," Jim said, as he hurried her along. "We still have about 10 miles to go."

"Ten miles," Cat said. "I'll never make it."

"You'll have to," Jim said and he grabbed her hand and pulled her along. Finally, they saw the border, but there were North Korean guards armed with high-powered rifles blocking their exit.

Jim dragged Cat behind a clump of trees just in time to avoid their being seen.

"What do we do now, Jim?" Mark asked.

"If we have a shoot out, it'll alert others. There's no way we can sneak across without being seen," Jim answered. "Cat, you stay here. Mark, you take the one on the left. I'll take the one on the right and try to get the other one before he can set off the alarm."

Mark caught the guard on the left and slit his throat before he could even see him. Jim did the same with the one on the right, then he caught the other one as he was escaping and eliminated him.

"Now, let's go. Run, Cat," Jim said, as he grabbed her hand and dragged her across the border just as several additional guards drove up.

Jim dived for cover and dragged Cat with him. Mark turned around and fired at the guards and then jumped behind the same cover. After several minutes of rapid gunfire, Jim said it was safe for them to continue further into South Korea.

When they were safely out of range of the North Koreans' gunfire, Jim said, "Come on. Let's get to a safer distance." When they were well away from the border, Jim tried to contact their drop chopper. After several tries, the pilot answered. Jim gave the pilot their location and soon he appeared. He hovered just long enough for Jim, Cat and Mark to board and then he took off again. After landing at the base in South Korea, they hurriedly boarded their C17 for home.

When they finally arrived back at the cabin, Jim asked Mark to come into his office with him.

"Mark, this thing you have for Cat," Jim started. "It's gotten out of hand. I know what you were thinking back there. Thank you for not doing it, but maybe it's best if you work with someone else for a while. Maybe just until you get your mind straight."

"Maybe you're right, Jim," Mark said. "I wouldn't have let you go. You know that, don't you? I admit it crossed my mind, but I couldn't have done it."

"Maybe not, but I just don't trust you right now," Jim said. "Why don't you try working with someone else for a while. When you think you're ready to work with me again, you can come back. You're never going to get Cat or my job as long as I'm alive, Mark," Jim said. "I know you don't think I deserve Cat, but she's my wife and she always will be. You may think I would have been unfaithful to Cat with Cassidy, but I never would have been."

"I can't help how I feel about Cat, Jim," Mark said. "It just happened. Maybe you're right. Maybe it would be best for me to be away from Cat for a while."

"Who do you want to work with, then?" Jim asked.

"Well, I really don't want to work with anyone else but you, but Don needs someone. I guess I can work with him for a while. Just a while, though. I don't think I could stand him for long," Mark answered.

"OK, I'll get the paperwork started," Jim said, as he picked up the phone to call Don Gardner.

For two months, Mark worked with Don Gardner's unit, which had assignments in North Korea occasionally and was temporarily stationed there. Jim tried to find a replacement for Mark, but there was always something wrong with the applicant, though. He hoped that Mark would soon get over his obsession with Cat and return to his team.

"What's wrong with this one?" Ted asked Jim one day when he had already turned down four other qualified applicants.

"He didn't do things the way I wanted them done," Jim answered.

"What you mean is he didn't do them the way Mark does. Isn't that right, Jim?" Ted asked angrily.

"Yeah, you're right. He didn't do it like Mark does. I taught Mark to do it the way I want it done. Mark did it the way I taught him," Jim answered.

"Well, then why don't you hire someone and teach them to do it the way you want it done?" Ted asked.

"Because I was hoping Mark would come back," Jim answered.

"I figured that was the problem all the time," Ted answered. "You don't need Mark back. You have me. You and Mark would just argue about Cat, anyway, if he did come back. Here. This is an application for Jason Hall. He has really good references. He's young enough that you can train him however you want him to be. Why don't you give him a try?" Ted asked, as he handed an application to Jim.

"OK, just to please you, I'll give him a chance," Jim answered.

Jim hired Jason Hall on a temporary basis to see how he worked out. He went on several missions with Jim and his team. Jim had finally decided that if Mark didn't come back, he would accept Jason as Mark's replacement.

Then the assignment that Jim dreaded taking without Mark came. An American diplomat, visiting South Korea, was kidnapped and taken to North Korea. The director gave Jim orders to go on the assignment, even though Don Gardner's team was still in South Korea working on another assignment but was short-handed.

Jim was pretty sure where they would be holding the diplomat and he dreaded making that raid again. They just barely got out with everyone the last time.

He called Cat into his office and told her that she would have to sit this one out.

"Why Jim?" Cat argued. "Why do I have to sit this one out? You know I'm capable of doing it."

"I know you can do it, Cat," Jim said. "I just don't want you to go this time. It's too dangerous."

"I've gone in dangerous situations before," Cat said. "Why can't I go this time?"

"Because I said so," Jim said angrily. "I don't want you to go and that's final."

When Jim was getting his gear ready to go, Cat ignored Jim's order and began getting her gear ready, too.

"I told you, you're not going," Jim said.

"You need me, Jim," Cat said, as she continued to get ready and ignored Jim's command. "You're already short-handed and besides,

I've been there before. I know what to expect and Jason's new. He doesn't know."

Finally, Jim gave in. He knew what Cat was saying was true. He just had an uneasy feeling about taking her with him this time. Even though it was against his better judgment, he allowed her to go.

It was harder than Jim had expected. The fighting was very intense. He took a shot in his left shoulder and began losing a lot of blood. Just as he was trying to get back out of range, he saw them capture Cat.

"No," he cried, and started toward her captors. Jason grabbed him and pulled him back. "Come on, Jim. We have to get to the chopper," Jason said, as he pulled Jim toward the hovering helicopter.

"Not without Cat," Jim said, as he pulled away from Jason.

"We'll come back for her," Jason said. "We can't get her now. You're in no shape to help her now, anyway. You've lost a lot of blood."

"I've got to get her," Jim said. He tried to pull away from Jason, but he was so weak from loss of blood that he almost passed out. Jason grabbed him and ran to the chopper. He shoved Jim aboard and jumped in himself. The chopper took off just in time. The North Koreans were hot on their tails and got several good shots at the chopper. One lucky shot hit the tail and made the chopper slew to the side, but the pilot got it under control and headed for the base in South Korea. At the base, Jim's wound was dressed and he was given a couple pints of blood.

The next day, he was ready to go back to get Cat.

"Jim, we can't go back, yet," Ted told him. We had several casualties. You'll have to wait until we can get some replacements."

"I can't wait, Ted," Jim said. "That's Cat over there. No telling what they'll do to her."

"You'll just have to wait. We can get Don's team. I think they're still here even though they are short-handed. They had some casualties on their last mission into North Korea, so they may have returned to the States.

"I can't wait, Ted," Jim said. "Get me my phone."

Jim called Mark's number. He didn't know if Mark would answer or if he and Don's team were still in South Korea or not, but he knew when he told Mark that Cat was in trouble, he would come as soon as possible.

"Hello, Jim," Mark said when he answered.

"Mark, Cat's been captured," Jim said without even saying hello.

"Where, when?" Mark asked immediately.

"Yesterday, in North Korea," Jim answered. "You know the same place. Mark, I need your help. I've lost most of my team. I have a new man, but he can't do it. I know you can. Will you come with me?"

"You know I will, Jim. Most of Don's team are down, though. It'll just have to be you and me," Mark said as he started getting ready to go.

"OK, that'll just have to do, then. Are you still in South Korea?" Jim asked.

"Yes, luckily we haven't gone yet because of the injuries. Where are you now?" Mark asked.

"I'm in the infirmary," Jim answered.

When Mark found Jim in the base infirmary, he saw Jim's arm in a sling.   "What's this?" he asked.

"I took a bad one," Jim said as he pulled the sling off and threw it on the ground. "Forget about that. I can do without it."

"Are you sure you can handle it, Jim?" Mark asked.

"I can handle it," Jim answered. "Let's go."

Jim and Mark fought their way into the compound and found Cat unconscious and chained to the floor like all the other prisoners they had rescued before.

"Cat, wake up," Jim said, as he slapped her face to get her to wake up.

She roused a little, but was unable to wake up. "They drugged her," Jim said. "I can't get her awake."

"Get her and let's go," Mark yelled. "Here they come."

"Cat, wake up. You've got to help me. I can't shoot and carry you at the same time," Jim begged. He pulled her to her feet, but she couldn't stand up, so he half dragged and half carried her.

Mark covered Jim and Cat until they got to the chopper. "Take Cat," Jim said to Mark. "I'll hold them off until you get airborne."

"Jim, you take Cat and let me cover you," Mark said. "You're already injured. Let me stay. You go."

"Do what I say," Jim shouted.

So Mark pulled Cat into the hovering chopper, as Jim waited and fired at the approaching North Koreans.

Mark leaned out and yelled "Take my hands, Jim." Jim grabbed Mark's hands with one hand and fired at the North Koreans with the hand of his injured shoulder. He was like a sitting duck hanging out of the chopper as Mark tried to pull him into the chopper. He took a number of bad shots before Mark could get him into the chopper.

"Jim," Cat cried, but she couldn't see because of the drugs that had her so groggy.

"I'm here, Hon," Jim said to her and then he looked at Mark. "Take care of her, Mark," he said weakly. "She's yours now. I'm not going to make it."

"I will take care of Cat, Jim, but you're going to make it," Mark said. Then Jim took a deep breath and stopped breathing. Mark started CPR on him immediately. There were so many wounds that blood was coming out faster than Mark could perform CPR on Jim.

"Come on, Jim, breathe," Mark said as he compressed Jim's chest. "Breathe, Jim," Mark said as he blew air into Jim's lungs. "Come on, Jim, don't you die on me," Mark said as he continued the CPR. "Breathe, dammit, Jim, breathe. Don't you dare die on me. Please, Jim. Please don't die." Mark started crying, "Breathe, dammit, Jim, breathe," he said as he continued to perform CPR.

Mark performed CPR on Jim until they reached the base in South Korea. With every compression and every breath, Mark said, "Breathe, Jim. Please breathe, Jim. Don't die. Please don't die. Breathe, dammit, Jim. Breathe." Mark was crying so hard now, he could hardly see, but he continued the CPR on Jim and begged him not to die. He continued CPR even though he was too exhausted to continue and he could see that the CPR was doing no good. He was crying so hard, he couldn't see through his tears. "Don't die, Jim," he cried. "Please don't die."

Mark was crying when they reached the base and Cat was still unconscious. Two medics jumped into the chopper and relieved Mark and continued CPR until they were certain it was no use to continue. They took Cat off and then carefully removed Jim's body.

Mark just stood and watched. He was crying so hard, he couldn't say anything.

There was nothing else he could say. Jim had said that he loved Cat more than life itself. He proved it by giving his life to save her.

"I wonder if I would have done the same thing," Mark thought. "Yes, I probably would have." Now, he would have to keep his promise to Jim. He would have to keep Cat safe.

He hurried into the ER behind the attendants carrying Jim's body. He was still hoping that he was wrong and Jim was still alive. He anxiously waited in the waiting room for a word about Jim and Cat.

Soon, the doctor came out and said, "I'm sorry. There was nothing we could do for Commander Ryan. He had just lost too much blood before you got here. There was just too much damage. His wife is still being treated. Someone will come get you when you can see her."

Mark sat down and cried until the nurse came and told him he could see Cat. As he walked down the hall to the examination room, he heard a scream and then "Nooooo. No, it can't be. No, no, no. He's not dead. Tell me you made a mistake. He can't be dead. I heard him. He told me he was there. He was safe. No, he's not dead. No, please tell me he's not dead. No, no, no. Please. Please don't let him be dead. Try again. He can't be dead."

Mark hurried on into Cat's room, just as the nurse was giving her a shot.

"Mark," she screamed, "Tell them Jim's OK. Tell them he's not dead. Tell them, Mark. Jim's OK. Tell them, Mark. Tell them."

Mark was crying so hard he couldn't say anything. He just held Cat's hand until the shot took affect.

When Mark was able to get himself under control, he called Carol, Cat's younger sister.

"Carol, this is Mark Fuller, Jim's friend," he began.

"Hi, Mark," Carol was surprised that Mark would call her. "What can I do for you?"

"I have some bad news to tell you," Mark said. Then he had to stop. He began crying again.

"What is it, Mark?" Carol was alarmed by Mark's tears. "Did something happen to Cat? What happened?"

"I'm sorry, Carol," Mark tried to finish telling her. "Jim's dead." That was all he could get out before he started crying again.

"What did you say, Mark?" Carol asked. "He can't be. I must have misunderstood you. What did you say?"

"I said, Jim is dead. Cat is in the ER now. We're at the base hospital in South Korea. I don't know how bad Cat is yet. I'll call you when I find out something."

"No, Mark, it can't be," Carol said. "How did it happen?"

"I can't talk right now, Carol," Mark said through his tears. "I just called to let you know. I'll call you again later. When I find out something. I've got to go now and check on Cat."

He knew that calling Carol before he knew for sure how Cat was probably was the wrong thing to do, but he had to call someone. He knew that he would have to call Ted, who had returned to the United States with the injured on Jim's team. He would also have to call the Director, but he couldn't right then. He had to go see if Cat was OK. When he found out for sure how she was doing, he would call Ted. Maybe Ted would call the Director and everyone else.

It was strange. Now, he had his wish. Cat was a widow and he would have a chance to win her love, and maybe he would be promoted to Commander of Jim's unit, but that didn't make him happy. All he felt was sadness. Sadness and deep despair. Whatever made him think he would be happy if Jim was gone? He certainly wasn't happy now.

He went back into the room to find Cat asleep. The shot had finally done what it was supposed to do. While he had been gone, they had taken her blood and taken some X-rays. They had dressed her wounds and started an IV.

After about an hour, the doctor said that he had gotten the results of all of the tests back. "She doesn't have any serious damage to any vital organs and she has no broken bones. It looks as if they are all superficial wounds. The drug in her system was something that was probably given to just knock her out so she would be easier to handle. We've dressed her wounds and given her something to make her sleep. We'll keep her here overnight and you can take her home in the morning."

"Thanks, Doc. I'll be out in the waiting room if you need me. I need to make some calls."

He called Carol again and she answered it after the first ring. "Carol, this is Mark again. Cat is in pretty fair condition. She had some superficial wounds and they have been dressed. She doesn't have any serious injuries and no broken bones. They had to give her a shot to make her sleep. She'll be here overnight and then I'll take her to the base in Washington. We'll probably stay there until she's checked out and then I'll bring her on home. Will you call Charlotte? I can't do that right now."

I've already called Charlotte, but I'll call her again and tell her what you said," Carol answered. "What happened, Mark? How did Jim die?"

"I'm sorry, Carol," Mark said, barely holding back his tears. "I just can't talk about it right now. I'll see you in a couple of days when we get home. I have to go now. I have some other calls to make."

"OK, Mark," Carol said. "Thanks for calling me."

Mark waited for a few minutes to get control of his emotions and then he called Ted. "Ted, this is Mark," he began. "Jim, Jim," then he stopped.

"Jim, what?" Ted asked. "Mark, what are you trying to tell me?"

"Jim didn't make it," Mark said before he started crying again.

"What do you mean, Jim didn't make it?" Ted asked, alarm in his voice.

"He and I went back to get Cat and Jim didn't make it back," Mark answered.

"You mean he's still over there?" Ted asked.

"No, I mean he's dead," Mark said.

Ted gasped. This was so sudden. He didn't even know Jim had gone back in to get Cat. He thought they were going to wait and get some replacements for the ones who were injured.

"When did he go back?" Ted wanted to know.

"We went last night, as soon as I could get ready," Mark said.

"Are you serious? Jim's really dead?" Ted asked.

"Yes, Ted, he's really dead," Mark answered. "Would you call the Director? I can't handle talking to him right now. Tell him I'll get him a report as soon as I can. Cat is injured. She has to stay here overnight, then we'll fly to Washington. We'll stop there for her to be checked out and then we'll fly home. I'll call him when I get home."

"Take your time, Mark," Ted said. "That report can wait for a while. We all know how close you and Jim were. Even though you were having some problems, I know you still cared a lot for each other."

"Yeah," Mark said. "I loved him like a brother. I'll really miss him."

"I know you will," Ted said. "So will we all."

The next morning, Mark checked Cat out of the hospital. He took her arm and started to lead her to a vehicle to be transported to one of the base planes. She stopped and refused to go any farther. "Mark, where's Jim?" she asked, determination in her voice.

"He's somewhere in the hospital, Cat," Mark answered, as he held her arm and tried to continue on to the vehicle with her.

"I want to see him," she insisted.

"You can see him when we get home. He isn't ready for you to see him now. You can see him after they get him ready at the funeral home," Mark answered, still trying to coax her toward the vehicle.

"I want to see him now," Cat said loudly. "I don't want to wait until we get home and they get him ready. Take me to see him now, Mark," she said jerking her arm out of Mark's grasp.

"You don't want to see him now, Cat. He isn't ready." Mark tried again to talk her out of seeing him.

"If you don't take me, I'll find someone else who will take me," Cat insisted. "I want to see him now."

"OK, I'll take you. Just let me find someone to take us to him," Mark said, as he started toward the nurse's station.

"I don't want them to do anything to him, either. I want to see him just as he is," Cat called after Mark.

"OK, Cat, wait here until I get back," Mark said, as he left Cat in the waiting room and went in search of someone to take them where Jim's body was waiting to be transported home.

He was told that Jim's body was in a holding room awaiting the transport back to the States. His body, after it had been processed, would be flown on the same plane in which Mark and Cat would be flying.

"His widow would like to see him before he is loaded onto the plane. Would it be possible for us to see him?" Mark asked when he was told where Jim's body was being held.

Mark was given permission to bring Cat to view Jim's body for a few minutes, so he went back to the waiting room to get her. He took her to the room where Jim was and one of the medical staff, who identified himself as Dr. Drew Marshall, led them to a metal drawer and opened it to reveal Jim lying there.

As they walked up to the place where Jim's body lay, Cat caught her breath. She started crying even before she could see Jim's body. Even with no life in him, he was still the most handsome man she had ever met. She leaned across his chest and sobbed uncontrollably, her body wracked in pain.

Mark and Dr. Marshall stood to the side and let her cry herself out. Then she touched the wounds that still had the blood stains on them. She caressed each wound and then she caressed his handsome face. "I love you, Jim," she said. "I'll always love you. I'll miss you so much. Why did you have to die? Why did you leave me? You told me you would never leave me. You promised."

Mark began to cry again. He didn't know how much more he could take. He prayed that God would comfort Cat soon. The only way he could find comfort himself, was if Cat could be comforted.

After about 15 minutes, Mark walked up to Cat and put his hand on her shoulder, "Cat, we need to go, now. We'll see him again at home when he's ready." He took her arm and led her out of the room. "Come on, let's go home," he said, as he led her out of the hospital and helped her into the waiting transport. The transport carried them to the airplane that would take them to the base hospital in Washington. They sat on the plane while Jim's body was loaded into the hold.

"You killed him, Mark. You killed Jim so you could have his job. You let him die," Cat said accusingly, as the airplane took to the air.

"No, Cat, I tried to save him," Mark said as he began to cry again. "He was just in too bad a shape. He had too many wounds. I couldn't stop the bleeding. I tried, Cat. I did my best."

"Your best wasn't good enough," Cat said. "He was OK when he got in the chopper. He told me. He said, 'I'm here, Hon.' He was OK. You killed him, Mark.

You just let him die. I hate you. I hate you."

"No, Cat, I didn't kill him," Mark was crying so hard now, he just sat beside her and cried. "I tried to save him, Cat. Believe me. I tried. I tried for as long as I could. He was just hurt too bad."

"Take me home, Mark, as soon as we get to Washington," Cat said. "I just want to go home. I don't need to wait until they check me out there. Just take me on to the Little Rock base and then drive me on home."

As they arrived at Little Rock AFB, Mark helped Cat into his personal vehicle that he had driven there when they made the trip to South Korea. Mark started the engine and pulled out of the parking lot. Cat sat on her side of the car as close to the door as possible. She never said anything else to Mark all the way home, so Mark drove all the way home in silence.

When they got home, Carol and Skip were waiting for them. Carol immediately threw her arms around Cat and Cat broke down in convulsive sobs. Mark headed straight for Jim's office to make his calls. He couldn't stand to see Cat cry anymore.

Ted and the other team members came soon after Mark called them. Ted went immediately into Jim's office with Mark.

"Did you call the Director?" Mark asked.

"Yes, I did. He said you could call him when you felt like talking," Ted answered.

"What will you do, now, Mark?" Ted asked.

"I don't know," Mark answered. "I'll just have to wait and see what happens."

Charlotte called and said that she and Tyler would be arriving that afternoon at 2:15. She asked if someone would be available to pick them up. Everyone, of course, volunteered.

After everyone had a chance to see Cat and tell her how sorry they were for her loss, Carol took her upstairs and put her to bed. Before they left the hospital in South Korea, the doctor had given Mark a prescription for some mild sedatives to help Cat sleep and Carol intended to make her take one.

"Carol, he's gone," Cat said. "What am I going to do? I can't live without him."

"Yes, you can, Cat," Carol said. "You still have your job and Mark will help you."

"Mark, Mark," Cat yelled at Carol. "Mark killed him. I know he did. Jim was OK when he got on the chopper. I talked to him. He knew it was me. He called me Hon. He was alive. Mark killed him."

"Cat, you don't know what you're saying," Carol tried to calm Cat down. "Mark loved Jim just like a brother. He would never kill him."

"I know he did," Cat said. "I hate him."

"No, you don't, Cat. You're just upset right now, but you don't hate Mark," Carol said. Then she got a glass of water and made Cat take one of the pills. Soon Cat was asleep and Carol went back downstairs. She went to the office door and knocked on it.

"Who is it?" Mark asked.

"It's me, Carol," she answered. "I need to talk to you."

"Come on in, Carol," Mark said.

As she came into the room, Ted said, "I'll be out in the den if you need me." Then he walked out and closed the door.

"Mark, I know Cat is just upset, but I want to know what happened," Carol said, as she sat down. "She says you killed Jim. What really happened."

"No, Carol, in answer to your question, I didn't kill Jim. He had lost too much blood. He had too many wounds. I tried to save him. I did CPR until I was so exhausted I couldn't do it any more. He never responded. He asked me to take care of Cat. I said I would and he, he just died."

Mark started to cry again. Telling what happened, brought it all back to him again, as if he was living it all over again.

"I'm sorry to have put you through that again, but I had to know," Carol said.

"Cat was taken prisoner," Mark began again. "Jim and I went alone to get her. I know that was a mistake, but Jim was insistent. He didn't want to wait for replacements for our injured men.

"When we got to her, she had been drugged and beaten. She was unconscious. Jim had already been wounded, so he was only using one arm. He told me to take Cat to the chopper and he would cover us. I got her inside and we took off. Jim was running to the chopper while shooting behind him. I took his hands and pulled him into the door of the chopper. He took several bad hits while he was getting in. Blood was everywhere. I've never seen so much blood. I started CPR, but the blood was coming so fast, I couldn't get any pulse. I tried, Carol. I did all I could do. He was just so far gone, I couldn't save him."

Carol was crying again as Mark told his story. Mark could hardly finish, he was crying also. "Thank you, Mark. I know that was hard for you. I won't make you tell it again. When Charlotte and Tyler come, I'll tell them, so you won't have to tell it again."

"Thanks, Carol," Mark said. "I'll probably have to tell it a lot more times before I'm through."

When Charlotte and Tyler arrived, Mark took them, along with Carol and Skip, into Jim's office. "I just wanted to tell you all how sorry I am," Mark said. "I wanted to let you know that Cat thinks I killed Jim. I know she's just upset, but I don't want you to believe what she's saying."

"That's OK, Mark," Charlotte said. "We know you wouldn't kill Jim. We know how much you thought of him. We know she's just upset. She has to blame someone and you're the nearest one."

"Anyway, I just wanted to see how you felt about me," Mark said.

"You know we think a lot of you, Mark, and we would never believe anything bad about you," Charlotte said, and the rest all agreed. Then Ted knocked on the door and said that Cat was looking for Mark, so Mark went to see what Cat wanted.

"Where is Jim, Mark? Has he arrived here yet?" Cat asked, when she saw Mark.

"He's at the funeral home now, Cat. They called while you were asleep to let me know that he has been taken there," Mark answered.

"I want to see him again," she insisted.

"You can see him tomorrow when he's ready," Mark answered.

"I want to see him now," Cat said. "I don't want to wait until tomorrow. Take me there now, Mark."

"You've already seen him once before he was ready, Cat. He's not ready. Why don't you wait until he's ready?" Mark tried to talk her out of it.

"If you don't take me, I'll get someone else to take me," Cat insisted. "I want to see him now."

"OK, I'll take you. Just let me call them first, so they'll be prepared," Mark said.

"No, I don't want them to do anything to him. I want to see him again just as he is," Cat said. "Now, take me or I'll find someone else who will."

"OK, Cat. Come on let's go," Mark said, as he took her arm and helped her to his vehicle.

"Cat, you know that Jim was my best friend," Mark said after he had driven out of the yard. "I would never do anything to intentionally hurt him. I loved him, Cat. He was like a brother to me. I couldn't have killed him," Mark pleaded for Cat to understand, but he felt he was pleading a losing case.

At the funeral home, Mark explained to the funeral director what Cat wanted to do. "That's highly unusual," the director said. "He isn't ready yet."

"I understand that, Sir, but she insists," Mark said. "Please just go along with her. She's been through a lot. She doesn't need any more trouble."

"OK, then. Come with me," the director said.

As they walked up to the place where Jim's body lay, Cat started crying again. Even though he had been gone for two days now, he was still the most handsome man she had ever met. His wounds had been cleaned and no longer had blood traces on them. She leaned across his chest and sobbed again, as she had done before they left the hospital in South Korea.

Mark asked the funeral director to stand to the side with him and let her cry herself out. She then gently touched each of his wounds again and caressed his handsome face. "I love you, Jim," she said. "I'll always love you. I'll miss you so much. Why did you have to die? I can't live without you. How will I ever be able to live without you?"

Mark began to cry again, too. He didn't know how much more he could take. He hated to see Cat cry. That was hurting him more than seeing Jim's body again. He prayed again that God would comfort Cat. He hoped that it would get easier for her to bear. If she could just stop crying so hard, it would be a lot easier on him.

After a few minutes, the funeral director asked Mark to see if he could get Cat to leave. He said they needed to finish getting Jim's body ready. Mark walked up to Cat and put his hand on her shoulder. "Cat, we need to go, now," he said. "We'll see him again when he's ready. Come on, let's go home."

Cat turned and gave Mark a look that could kill, but she let him lead her away. She kept looking back, though, as if she thought Jim might get up. She still couldn't accept the fact that he was really gone.

When they got back to the cabin, their friends and neighbors were there to offer their condolences. Cat gave them a weak smile and said, "Thank you for coming. I'm sorry, but I have to go upstairs. Please forgive me." Then she hurried up the stairs.

The next morning, Mark told Cat that they had an appointment with the funeral director to make Jim's arrangements. "We'll go right after breakfast," he said. "Do you want Carol and Charlotte to go with us?"

"I guess," Cat said without feeling. "It really doesn't matter."

Mark called Carol and asked if she and Charlotte wanted to go with them.

"Yes, Mark," Carol answered. "We would like to be with Cat when she makes the arrangements."

"I'll swing by and pick you up in a few minutes, then," he said.

After Mark picked up Carol and Charlotte, they made the trip to the funeral home in silence. The only sound was Cat sniffling every now and then.

Cat sat in the funeral director's office with a blank look on her face. She looked as if all feeling had been drained out of her. When the director asked her how she wanted something, she said she didn't care. Carol and Charlotte would suggest something and she said it was OK with her, whatever they thought. "Carol, it doesn't matter. He's gone. That's all that matters to me. You and Charlotte just do what you think is best. I can't do this. Mark, please take me home." So Carol and Charlotte hurriedly finished the arrangements and hurried out to the car where Cat and Mark were waiting.

When they arrived back at the cabin, Cat went upstairs and Carol and Charlotte visited with their friends.

The funeral was scheduled for 2:00 p.m. on Wednesday afternoon. Barbara prepared lunch and had it ready to eat at noon. Everyone, except Cat and Mark, ate when it was ready. Cat and Mark sat in the den waiting until time to leave for the funeral home.

The funeral home was packed. There was a large representation of FSC agents and commanders, as well as friends and neighbors. Director Halbert was also there. Their pastor, Rev. Miller, from Landmark Baptist Church, preached the funeral. He told how he had known Jim since he was a small boy. He had always been a kind and considerate person and had accepted Jesus as his Savior at an early age. Rev. Miller said that he knew that Jim would be sorely missed by his family, friends and co-workers. He said that God had Jim's mansion ready, so He had called him home.

"Mark Fuller, Jim's best friend and Second-in-Command, has a poem he would like to read at this time," Rev. Miller said. Then he called Mark up to the podium.

"I found this beautiful poem written by David Romano. I feel that it describes the type of person Jim was. It's a little long, but I would like to read it for you now. The name of the poem is *When Tomorrow Starts Without Me* by David M. Romano. It begins like this:

> When tomorrow starts without me and I'm
> not there to see,

If the sun should rise and find your eyes all
filled with tears for me;
I wish so much you wouldn't cry the way you
did today,
While thinking of the many things, we didn't
get to say.

As Mark read the beautiful poem, his eyes were filled with tears and he could hardly speak, but he finally read the beautiful ending to the poem:

So when tomorrow starts without me, don't
think we're far apart,
For every time you think of me, I'm right
here, in your heart.*
*Copyright David M. Romano December 1993

Mark was barely able to read the last few lines because of the lump in his throat. He finished reading and hurried to his seat before he started crying in front of everyone.

"Thank you, Mark, for that beautiful poem," Rev. Miller said. Then he read some comforting scriptures and had a word of prayer. He closed the service and stood beside Jim's casket as their friends filed past. After all of their friends had filed past Jim's casket and into the hallway, the funeral director closed the doors and let Cat and her family have some alone time with Jim.

Cat walked up to Jim's casket, fell across his chest and began sobbing. Her body was again wracked by the convulsive sobs. "No, Jim. Please don't leave me," she sobbed. Mark let her sob for a while, then he put his arm around her and urged her toward the door.

When they returned to the cabin after the funeral, Cat again went upstairs. Carol and Charlotte followed her. "Cat, you need to eat something," Carol said.

Cat just looked at Carol with a blank stare, as if she couldn't comprehend what Carol was saying.

"Please, Cat, eat something," Charlotte said.

"Just leave me alone," Cat said. "I don't want anything to eat. I just want to die and go with Jim."

"Don't say that, Cat," Carol said. "We don't want you to die. Please eat something for us."

"I don't want anything. Just go away and leave me alone," Cat shouted at them and threw herself onto the bed and began sobbing again. They decided it would probably be best to do as she said, so they went back downstairs.

"Mark," Carol said, when she got his attention. "Maybe you can get her to eat something."

"I learned a long time ago that you don't make Cat do something she doesn't want to do," Mark said. "Jim couldn't even make her do what he said, if she didn't want to do it. I'll go up and see what I can do, though."

He went on up the stairs and knocked on the door. "Cat, can I come in?" he asked. She didn't answer, so he opened the door a crack. He saw her sitting on the bed staring straight ahead. He came into the room and sat on the bed next to her.

"Your sisters are worried about you, Cat," he said. "They think you need to eat something."

"I don't want to eat anything," Cat said. "I just want to die and go be with Jim."

"Cat, Jim didn't give his life just so you could die. He died so you could live. You dishonor his sacrifice for you, if you just let yourself die. He wanted you to live."

She gave Mark a look of pure hatred and said, "Go away, Mark. I hate you. You let him die. I know you just let him die, so you could get his job."

"No, Cat, I tried to save him. I didn't let him die," Mark said, hurt by Cat's words. It felt as if she had stabbed him in the heart with a knife.

"Go away, Mark," she said. "I don't even want to see you ever again."

"Cat, you don't know what you're saying," he answered. "You're hurting right now, but it'll get better."

"No, it won't, Mark," she said. "Just go away and leave me alone."

He decided it would be better to leave her alone right then. Maybe it would get better.

After everyone was gone, Mark decided to check on Cat. He knocked on the door again, but he still didn't get a response. He cracked the door a little and looked inside. Cat was still sitting where she had been earlier and still staring into space.

He went back downstairs and got a glass of water and one of Cat's pills, then went back up to her room. He knocked on the door again, but still no response. He slowly opened the door.

"Cat, I brought you a pill," he said. "You need to take it. You'll feel better."

"I don't want to feel better and I don't want the pill," she said

"Please take the pill, Cat," he said, as he held it out to her.

"I don't want the pill and I don't want to ever see you again," she said.

"OK, Cat, I'll just set the water and the pill here on the nightstand, if you decide you want it." Then he went back downstairs.

CHAPTER 15

Carol and Skip were going to begin teaching school in a few weeks. It was their first year to teach. They were excited about starting to school, but they were worried about leaving Cat alone while they were gone. Charlotte and Tyler were working on a new movie and would have to be going back to Hollywood soon.

Mark was trying to get Jim's unit back together again. Some of them were still recuperating from their wounds, so he didn't know when he would be taking on a new assignment.

After two weeks, he finally had a rag-tag group of men. Jason was becoming a valuable member of his team, but he was hoping that Cat would soon be able to take her rightful place again. He hadn't gotten the official word that he had been promoted to Commander yet, but he hoped it would come before he had to take the team on an assignment.

Cat came out of her room occasionally to eat a little bit and went back upstairs again. Charlotte spent as much time as she could with her before she had to go back to Hollywood and Carol spent what time she could with her. They each tried to coax her into going outside or at least going downstairs.

One day, Carol got her to take a walk over to their cabin. As soon as they walked into the cabin, Cat began to sob. She went up to the fireplace and said, "We got married right here. This is where he promised me he would be with me forever."

"What a mistake," Carol thought, as she urged Cat back to her cabin.

After Charlotte and Tyler left and Carol and Skip had started teaching, Mark decided to try to get Cat out of her room again.

"Come on down to the office, Cat," he said. "I'm planning an assignment. I need your help."

"No," Cat said with that hateful look again. "I never want to go into that room ever again. I want you to get all of the FSC stuff out of my house, too. I'll give you four days to get it out of here. I want you out, too. Get all of your gear and your personal stuff out of here. I never want to see you or FSC ever again."

"Cat, you don't mean that," Mark said incredulously.

"Yes, I do," Cat said. "I want everything that belongs to FSC out of Jim's office and I want all of your belongings out of your room by Monday."

"OK, Cat, I'll get it out. I can get an office in the FSC building and I can get a bed in the barracks, but I need you on my team. I'm short-handed. I really could use you."

"I'm never going to be on your team. I told you. I never want to have anything to do with FSC again. The FSC took the person I loved most in all the world. I could have had a wonderful marriage, if it hadn't been for the FSC. I hate you Mark Fuller. Do you understand. I hate you and I hate the FSC. I never want to see you again. Now go away and leave me alone."

November 21 was getting close and Carol and Skip were planning a special outing to celebrate their wedding anniversary. They were afraid to mention it to Cat, but they hated not to invite her. Carol finally decided to tell Cat and let her decide what she wanted to do.

"Cat, you know November 21 will be here soon, don't you?" Carol asked Cat.

"Yes, I know," Cat answered, hardly blinking an eye.

"Skip and I are going out to eat, would you like to come with us?" Carol cautiously asked.

"No, Carol," Cat said. "I have no reason to celebrate that date anymore. Please don't ever ask me again."

"I'm sorry, Cat," Carol said with tears in her eyes. "I didn't want to leave you out."

"Please, Carol," Cat said. "Just leave me out of everything from now on. I don't want to be a part of anything."

"Come on, Cat," Carol said. "You don't mean that. Thanksgiving will be here soon and we should celebrate together like we always did."

"I have nothing to be thankful for, Carol," Cat said. "I won't be celebrating Thanksgiving, either."

"I thought you and Mark might at least come and eat with Skip and me. I think Charlotte and Tyler will be here, too. We can all be together again."

"If I even considered coming to your Thanksgiving celebration, I wouldn't invite Mark Fuller. I have nothing to do with that man anymore. I don't even want to hear his name again."

"Come on, Cat, Mark didn't do anything to Jim. He just tried to save him. You should be thankful that he tried to save him," Carol pleaded.

No, he didn't try to save him," Cat said. "He killed him. I never want to see or hear from that man again."

So Thanksgiving came and went and Christmas came and went and Cat stayed mostly in her room alone.

On New Year's Day, Cat decided to go down to the den and watch the New Year's Day Parade on the TV there. The phone rang and when she answered it, it was Mark.

"Hi, Cat," he said.

"I don't want to talk to you, Mark," she said. "Just leave me alone."

"I need to see you, Cat," he said. "Please let me come see you."

"I don't want to see you," Cat said.

"Just for a few minutes, Cat," Mark pleaded.

"OK," Cat finally gave in. "I'll see you for a few minutes."

Shortly, there was a knock at the door. When she opened it, Mark was standing there.

"Come on in," Cat said, as she led him to the den. "Sit down."

"I just had to see you, Cat," Mark started. "I know you think it was my fault that Jim died, but it wasn't, Cat. I tried to save him. Believe me, I tried. He had so many wounds. The blood was coming faster than I could do CPR. I did CPR until I was completely exhausted, but it did no good. I loved Jim like a brother. I couldn't have killed him."

"Maybe you did try to save him, but why didn't you stay and let him get in the chopper first? He was already wounded. He should have gone first and you should have stayed and covered us. Why didn't you?"

"Because Jim ordered me to take you and go to the chopper," Mark said. "He said he would cover us. He ordered me, Cat. I have always obeyed Jim's orders. I may not have always liked one of his orders, but I always obeyed them. He was the boss and I knew it. Cat, I need you back on my team."

"Your team," Cat said angrily. "It's already your team, then?"

"I haven't gotten the official word, yet, but I've been doing the Commander duties. Some of the men don't like it, though. Ted feels that he should be Commander because he's been here longer than I have, but I was Jim's Second-in-Command. It stands to reason that I would take over as Commander."

"I guess that's the logical conclusion," Cat said without any feeling for or against it.

"Cat, please come back," Mark pleaded. "I really do need you. You were one of the best. I've tried several other women, but it didn't work out. I had Jenny try for a while. You remember Jenny, don't you?" When Cat said she remembered her, Mark continued. "Jenny didn't like taking orders from me. She said I wasn't the official Commander, so she didn't have to take orders from me. We had our personal problems, anyway, so that didn't work out.

"I've tried several male applicants, but they didn't work out either. I guess Jim spoiled me. He taught his team to do things the way he wanted them done and I guess I expect everyone to be taught the way Jim taught. It doesn't work out like that, though. There's no one else like Jim."

"I know," Cat said and she began to cry.

"I'm sorry, Cat. I didn't mean to make you cry," Mark said. He started to put his arm around Cat's shoulders, but she pulled away from him.

"I'm really sorry, Cat," Mark said, as he backed away from Cat. "I guess I shouldn't have come. I just thought I could persuade you to come back to the unit."

"No, Mark," Cat said. "I'll never go back to the unit. I only became a member so I could be close to Jim. Now that he's gone, there's no reason for me to be a member."

"I guess I had better go, then," he said, as he walked toward the door. "Cat," he said hesitantly, as he turned toward Cat. "Have you been back to church since Jim's death?"

"No," Cat said sharply. "I don't want to go to church anymore. God deserted Jim, so I don't see any reason to go to church anymore."

"Cat," Mark swallowed hard and then said, "Would you go with me Sunday?"

"No, Mark, I will not go to church with you," Cat said.

"Please, Cat, just try it with me one time," Mark pleaded. "If you're uncomfortable when we get there, I'll just bring you back home."

"I said no, Mark. That's my final answer."

"Goodbye, Cat, I hope you're able to forgive me someday," Mark said. Then he opened the door and left.

Cat sat down on the sofa and sobbed. "Why did he come here?" she asked of no one. "I hate him. I hate him. I hate him. Why doesn't he leave me alone?"

That Sunday morning, about 10:00 a.m., there was a knock on the door. "Who can that be?" Cat wondered. When she opened the door, she was surprised to find Mark standing there. He was dressed in a dark blue suit with a blue tie and shirt. Cat was impressed at how handsome he looked in spite of herself.

"Mark," she said. "What are you doing here?"

"I thought I would try again to get you to go to church with me. Will you come go with me?"

Cat couldn't help but laugh at Mark's audacity. "Mark, I can't believe you," she said, as she opened the door wider so he could come inside.

"OK, if you're determined to take me to church, sit down for a few minutes while I get dressed," Cat said, as she ran upstairs to change clothes.

When she came back down, Mark's heart skipped a beat. She was the beautiful Cat that he had fallen in love with. The disapproving frown was gone and there was a warm smile in its place.

"OK, Mark, we better go before I change my mind," she said.

Mark took her arm and led her to his car and helped her get inside. After he took his seat behind the wheel and fastened his seat belt, he said. "We don't have to go to the church where you and Jim went, if it's too hard on you. There's a little Baptist church just a few miles from here where we can go, if you would like.

"OK," Cat said. "Let's go there. I don't think I could go where Jim and I went. There are too many memories."

So they went to the little Baptist church down the road. When they walked into the church, everyone was surprised to see two strangers, but it didn't take them long to welcome them to the service. Everyone offered them a hymnal and asked if they needed anything else. Soon, Cat relaxed and, when the preacher started his sermon, she enjoyed it in spite of herself.

After the service, everyone shook their hands and told them they were glad they had come. "Please come back again," the preacher said. "We were glad to have you."

Cat said, "Thank you," and hurried out and got into Mark's car, but Mark stood and talked to the preacher for a few minutes.

"Would you like to go get something to eat before you go home?" Mark asked. He wanted to keep her with him as long as he could.

"No, Mark, I just want to go home," Cat said. "I don't eat much these days. It would just be a waste."

When they got back to the cabin, Cat said, "Mark, I enjoyed being with you today, but I don't want to see you again. It's too painful. Please don't come back." Then she shut the door in his face and ran up the stairs and threw herself on the bed and sobbed.

Mark was deeply crushed. He had thought that he was finally getting through the wall that Cat had built between them. He decided that it was no longer any use to try to get through to her. The wall was too thick and there were too many bad memories connected to it. He decided that it wasn't meant for him to have a life with Cat, so he might as well give up.

CHAPTER 16

The cold, dreary January days finally dragged into February and Cat started getting outside a little at a time. She planted flowers and sat out in the sunshine on days when the sun was warm and the cold wind didn't blow. She thought about how much she liked the little Baptist church where Mark had taken her, so she went again and everyone was just as friendly as they had been the first time. Her heart was beginning to melt a little at a time, as the weather began to warm into Spring.

One morning, she decided to call Bill Hawkins, the editor of the paper where she worked before she and Jim were married. "Bill, this is Cat Ryan," she said, when Bill answered the phone.

"Hi, Cat," Bill said. "I'm sorry about your husband. I meant to call, but I just put it off and after a while, it just seemed like it was too late. You know how it is."

"That's OK, Bill," Cat said. "I didn't feel like talking to anyone, anyway. What I called about is, I have a lot of time on my hands now and I wondered if you had an opening I could fill. Just something part-time would be good. I just need to get out of the house."

"You're in luck, Cat," Bill said. "My feature writer just resigned. I was just going to advertise it. Would you be interested in that? It would probably just be a part-time position."

"Yes, I would definitely be interested in it," Cat said happily.

"OK, then, come by my office about 9:00 a.m. Monday morning and we'll talk salary and hours."

"Thanks, Bill, I really appreciate it," Cat said.

So, on Monday morning, Cat went to see Bill Hawkins. He immediately hired her and told her she could start the following Monday.

She could hardly wait to get home and tell Carol. Carol was so glad that Cat was finally coming out of her depression.

After she had worked at the paper for a few weeks, she was even willing to go shopping with Carol. One day, Carol asked Cat to go to an infant's fashion shop. "Why do you want to go here?" Cat asked.

"Because, Cat," Carol said with a grin on her face. "You're going to be an aunt."

"Oh, Carol," Cat said joyfully. "You're going to have a baby. I'm so happy for you and Skip. When is it due?"

"It should be here sometime around the middle of October, maybe even the first part of October."

"That's great," Cat said. Then she started feeling sad. Jim had wanted children. He had already asked her to think about having a baby. He said his biological clock was ticking and he wanted to have them while he was still young enough to enjoy them. Now, he never would get that chance.

"I think I'll just wait in the car," Cat said. "I think I'm more tired than I thought."

"I hope I don't get like this every time someone tells me they're expecting," Cat thought. "Charlotte may even be next. That would really devastate me."

Carol had a baby girl on October 15. They named her Sherry Rene. Cat was so proud to be her aunt and to have her named Rene after her. She spent as much time with her as she could. She felt that she was the prettiest baby girl she had ever seen.

Cat had started volunteering at the local children's hospital in her spare time. Between her job at the paper, her volunteering and her role as Sherry's aunt, Cat was so busy she didn't even notice the passing of time. Before she knew it, three years had passed. She still had periods of depression when she stopped to think about what her life would have been if Jim had lived. She still missed him so much that it hurt, but the hurt was slowly beginning to ease up.

She was working on a feature story at the paper office one morning when a photograph with another story caught her eye. The picture was of a handsome man, dressed in a suit and tie. His hair was combed neatly, except for one lone strand that wanted to fall down over his right eye. He looked so familiar to her that she stopped what she was doing to read the article. The name under the picture was Unit Commander Mark Fuller of the Federal Security Commission (FSC). Her heart skipped a beat when she saw his name. She hurriedly read the article.

"Unit Commander Mark Fuller was seriously injured last night when he and his unit raided an alleged terrorist compound. Commander Fuller is now in the IC Unit at the Baptist Hospital East."

The article went on to tell how Mark and his team had been doing surveillance on the compound for months. When they thought they had enough evidence, they raided the compound. There was an accident and somehow the bomb exploded as Mark and his team entered the building.

"I need to go see him," Cat thought. "Will he even want to see me after what I said to him the last time I saw him."

Cat left the paper office early and went by the hospital. She went to the ICU and asked about Commander Mark Fuller.

"Are you a member of his immediate family or a relative of Mr. Fuller?" the attendant asked.

"No, I'm just a close friend," she answered.

"What is your name?" she was asked.

"Catherine Ryan," Cat answered.

"I'm sorry, but your name isn't on the visitor's list. You will need to talk to Mr. Fuller's relatives to get that information. We aren't allowed to give information to anyone who isn't on the list," the attendant rattled off, as if she knew the spiel by heart.

"Who is on his list, then?" Cat asked.

"I'm sorry, but I can't give you that information, either."

"Thank you," Cat said and then she left.

Cat tried the number of the FSC office and asked for Ted Ames, but she got nowhere there, either.

"I guess I'll just have to wait until he's out of ICU," Cat thought.

Cat waited a week and decided to try again. "Maybe he'll be in a regular room and I can go see him," she thought.

This time, luck was with her. Mark had been transferred to a regular room and when she asked for his room number, she was able to obtain it. She found that he was on the fourth floor, so she caught the elevator and went up to the fourth floor. She found his room and tapped on the door. A nurse opened the door and asked if she could help Cat.

"I'm a friend of Commander Fuller. May I see him," she asked.

"Just a minute. Let me check," she said and then she asked Mark if he felt like having a visitor.

"Sure," he said. "Who is it?"

Cat walked up to Mark's bed. She caught her breath when she saw how he was bandaged. His eyes were covered with thick bandages held together with tape. His right arm was in a sling and there was a cast on his right leg.

"Who is it?" Mark asked again. "I can't see anything. You'll just have to say who you are."

"It's Cat, Mark," Cat said, as she walked closer to the bed.

"Cat," he said, as his heart skipped a beat. "I never thought I'd ever see you again. Well, I guess I'm not seeing you now, either." Then he gave a little chuckle. He held out his left hand and Cat took it in both of hers.

"How are you, Cat?" he asked.

"Better than you, it looks like," Cat said.

"You wouldn't have to be very well to be better than I am," he answered.

"How did you find out I was here?" he asked.

"I read about it in the newspaper," Cat answered.

"Oh, I didn't think about that. I thought maybe Ted might have called you," he answered. "I guess I should have known he wouldn't. It's been a long time, Cat."

"Yes, it has been, Mark," Cat said. "How long before you get out of the hospital?"

"I don't know for sure. Maybe a week or two," Mark answered.

"Where will you go when you get out?" Cat asked.

"To a nursing home, I guess, if I can't see when they take these bandages off. The doc said there's a fifty/fifty chance that I won't get my eyesight back. I can't stay at the barracks like this. It'll probably be best if I stay in a nursing home for a while. At least until I get rid of this thing on my leg.

"I can't feel sorry for myself," he continued. "It's my own damn fault. Jim always told us to make sure there wasn't a trap before we went tearing into a building. I was in a hurry. I wanted to make sure they didn't get away. After all that time Jim kept pounding it into my head, I still didn't do the right thing. Boy, I wish Jim was still here. If he had been with us, I wouldn't be in this shape."

Cat had to choke back tears at the mention of Jim's name. It still hurt thinking about how much she missed him.

"Cat, are you still here?" Mark asked.

"Yes, I'm here," Cat had trouble talking with the lump in her throat. "I have to go now, though. I'll come back tomorrow and maybe I can stay longer."

"I'll look forward to it, Cat. Thanks for coming," he said.

Cat took his hand and gave it a squeeze. "Bye for now, Mark."

"Bye, Cat. Come back anytime," he said.

Cat went again the next day and every day for the two weeks before his bandages were removed.

She found out what books he liked and she would read to him for hours at a time. She brought CD's with the kind of music he liked and played them for him. Then the day came for his bandages to be removed.

"Cat," Mark told her. "I want you to stand there, right at the foot of the bed. I want you to be the first thing I see, if I can see anything."

Cat stood at the foot of the bed praying that he would be able to see. She wondered what would happen to him, if he was never able to see again. How would he be able to live? Would anyone take care of him? Would anyone even care for him or care whether he lives or dies? She held her breath and waited for the bandages to be removed.

This is the end of Part 1 of the Unit Commander. Turn the page for an exciting sneak peek at Part 2 of the Unit Commander - Mark Fuller's Story Book 2 of the FSC series.

CHAPTER 1
PART 2 - MARK
FULLER'S STORY

Doctor Sanders removed the bandages from Mark Fuller's eyes slowly, layer by layer. When all of the gauze was gone and only the pads directly on his eyes remained, Dr. Sanders said, "I want you to shut your eyes now, and open them slowly."

Mark shut his eyes and began to open them slowly, as the doctor had said. The light hurt at first and he blinked. Then he opened them again. There was a smoky haze there, but he could tell that there was light shining through the haze. Then he could see a shadow at the foot of the bed where Cat had positioned herself at Mark's request.

"Can you see anything," Dr. Sanders asked.

"Only shadows," Mark answered. "I know Cat is standing there, but I can't see her."

"Close your eyes again and open them slowly again," the doctor said.

Mark did as Dr. Sanders asked. Still he could see only shadows.

"I can still only see shadows," Mark said, showing his disappointment.

"Maybe it'll clear up in a few days," the doctor said. "If it doesn't, then I'm afraid you'll never be able to see again."

Mark took a deep breath and sighed, "I guess I deserved that.

It's my own fault. I should have been more careful when we raided the alleged terrorist house."

"Don't get so discouraged so soon," Dr. Sanders said. "I've seen it take up to two weeks sometimes. We'll just give it time. I've prescribed some drops for you to use four times a day. That may help. It doen't hurt to try anyway. I'm also giving you a prescription for an antibiotic. You are to take it four times a day. Be sure and take all of them or they won't do you any good. Here is also a prescription for pain medication. You'll need that for a while."

Then he turned to Cat, "Will you be taking him home, Miss?" he asked.

"Yes, probably," Cat answered.

"Then, here are some instructions for you. Please follow them exactly or he could get an infection. That would really be bad."

He gave Cat the instructions and she put them into her purse. "Do you want to go home with me, Mark?" she asked.

"Sure, if my other choice is the nursing home. I'll take your place any day," Mark answered.

"OK, that's settled," the doctor said. "The nurse will be here to discharge you shortly. I'll leave an appointment for you. I want to see you in my office in one week. After the cast comes off in a few weeks, you'll be set up for some therapy. Is there anything you want to know?"

"The only thing I really want to know is if I'll ever be able to see again, but you've already answered that, so I guess there's nothing else I need to know. Do you have any questions, Cat?"

"No, I guess not. I have these instructions and, if I have any problems, I'll just call the doctor's office."

"That's right, Miss," Dr. Sanders said. "If there are no other questions, then I'll see you in a week. Be safe." Then he left and the nurse came in to discharge Mark. Cat went on downstairs to get the car while the nurse pushed Mark down in a wheelchair.

After the nurse loaded Mark into Cat's car, Cat went around and got into the driver's seat. "Do you feel like stopping long enough to have your prescriptions filled or do you want me to take you home and come back for them?" Cat asked Mark, as she started the engine.

"There's not any sense in your making another trip back to town for my meds. I'll just wait while you have them filled," Mark answered.

When Cat got to the pharmacy, she asked Mark if he wanted to go in with her. Since it was a beautiful Fall-like day, he said he would just wait for her in the car.

Cat hurried into the pharmacy and turned in his prescriptions. When they were ready, the cashier asked for Mark's birthdate. Cat had no idea what Mark's birthdate was. "I'm sorry," she said. "I'm picking these up for a friend. I can't remember his birthdate. He's waiting in the car. He has had an injury to his eyes and doesn't feel like coming in."

"I'm sorry," the cashier said. "I can't let you have these without the proper identification. Can he either come in or give you his ID?"

"He isn't in any shape to come in," Cat said. "I'll get his ID, if that's all you need."

When she arrived back at the car, Mark was asleep. She hated to awaken him, but she had no other choice. She shook him gently and called his name. He awoke with a start.

"I'm sorry to have to awaken you, Mark, but I need your ID," Cat said.

"Oh, I should have given it to you," Mark said grogily. "I should have known you would need it. Here it is," he said, handing it to Cat, after a search through all of his pockets finally revealed it in his shirt pocket.

Cat took the ID he handed to her and noticed it was his FSC ID. She noticed that it didn't contain his birthdate. "Mark, I need your driver's license, if you have it. This doesn't have your birthdate on it."

"It's October 15, 1985," he said.

Cat gave him a strange look, but just said "Do you have your driver's license? I know it has it on it."

Mark moved around painfully and tried to find his wallet in his back pocket, but he gave up because of the pain. "I can't find it, Cat. I don't know where it is. It must be in some of my things. Just give them that and tell them my birthdate. Maybe that will satisfy them."

So Cat made the trip back into the pharmacy armed with Mark's ID and his birthdate. This time, she was successful. When she got back to the car, Mark was asleep again.

She got into the car as quietly as she could, but when she closed the door, Mark jumped. "I'm sorry, Mark, I didn't mean to awaken you. Are you all right?" she asked as she handed him the medicine and his ID card.

"Yes, I'm OK. I think the pain shot that the nurse gave me before I left the hospital has finally taken effect," he said. "I hope I can get out of the car when we get to your place."

When Cat pulled up in front of the cabin and stopped, Mark awoke with a start again.

"We're here, Mark," Cat said, and she walked around the car and opened the door for Mark. "Put your arm around my shoulders and use your crutch. Maybe we can make it into the house without falling down. At the door, she braced Mark against the wall while she unlocked and opened the door.

"Do you want to lie down on the sofa in the den?" Cat asked.

"Yes, that would be fine," Mark answered.

Cat helped Mark to the sofa and he fell onto it. "That was a chore," Mark said.

"Was it as hard for you as it was for me?"

"It was hard," Cat chuckled as she answered. "Maybe it'll get easier after we practice for a while. You just lie down and I'll bring your things in. Do you want me to put them in your room upstairs or do you want them down here?" Cat asked, as she headed for the door.

"If you don't mind, I'd like to stay down here for a while. I hate tackling those stairs already."

"Sure, you can stay down here as long as you feel you need to." Then she disappeared and reappeared shortly with his things.

"Mark, I'll put your things right over here, so they'll be handy for you, but they'll be out of the way," Cat said, as she picked a spot that would be easy for Mark to get to, but wouldn't be in his way.

"Are you hungry?" Cat asked after she got Mark settled.

"I could eat something, but don't go to any trouble," he said.

"I've made some vegetable beef soup and cornbread muffins. I like soup and cornbread on cool nights like this. Is that OK with you?"

"That would be fine," Mark answered. Then he lay back on the pillow that Cat had given him and went to sleep again.

Cat went into the kitchen and put the soup on the stove to heat and placed bowls and spoons onto the table.

When it was ready, she helped Mark to the table. She said a short prayer and then filled Mark's and her bowls with the steaming hot soup. "Cat, do you mind directing me to the bowl," Mark said a little embarrassed. "I can't tell for sure where it is and I don't want to make a mess."

"That's OK, Mark, let me help you," Cat said, as she took Mark's hand and directed it to the bowl. "Would you like for me to help you?" she asked when she saw that he was still having a difficult time.

"That would be great," Mark answered. So Cat sat next to Mark and helped him eat. "Would you like some dessert?" she asked. "I have a pecan pie."

"I'm pretty full, but I can't pass up pecan pie," Mark answered. "Just give me a small piece."

Cat cut Mark a small piece of pie and helped him eat it. "That was very good, Cat. I didn't know you could cook," Mark said, as he patted his stomach.

"Thanks," Cat said. "When Molly and Barbara were cooking for us, I had no reason to cook. Now that I'm the only one here, I didn't see any reason for Barbara to cook for only one person. I told her she might as well leave, if she wanted to go somewhere else. She's working at the hunting lodge now. They have groups that come in during hunting season. She enjoys cooking for a lot of people, so she's happier there. She comes and visits me every now and then."

Then Cat went to the stove and dipped up a container of soup and put some cornbread muffins into a plastic bag. "I fix dinner for Carol sometimes, when I have time. It helps her out. She teaches at the high school in town and comes home exhausted. She has a little girl. She will be three years old this month. As a matter of fact, her birthday is October 15, also. Do you remember my sister, Carol?"

"Yes, I remember Carol. Wow, that's a coincidence about our birthdays, isn't it?" Mark said, amazed at the coincidence.

"Let me help you back to the sofa," Cat said. "Then I'll clean up the kitchen."

"Can't I stay here while you do that?" Mark asked. "I would really like to talk to you while you do that."

"Sure, you can stay," Cat answered. "I just thought you might need to rest."

Then there was a knock on the door. When Cat answered it, Carol came rushing into the room. "Gee, it's beginning to get cold out there," she said. "I didn't know it was supposed to turn this cold so soon."

"Why didn't you wear a jacket?" Cat asked.

"I didn't realize it was so cold," Carol said, as she headed toward the kitchen, but she stopped when she saw Mark.

"Who's that?" she mouthed without saying a word.

"Carol, do you remember Mark Fuller?" Cat said, as she urged Carol toward Mark. "He was Jim's Second-in-Command, remember?"

"Oh, yeah, I remember him," Carol said. "What happened to you, Mark?"

"Hi, Carol," Mark said, as he held out his hand in Carol's direction. "I had an accident. Your wonderful sister was kind enough to volunteer to help me get well."

"Yeah, Cat's really kind like that," Carol said frowning. "She's always taking in strays; a stray cat here, a stray dog there. Now, I guess she's taken in a stray person."

"Yes, that's me," Cat said. "I'm a very compassionate person. Now, Carol, don't you need to get this soup home before it gets cold?"

"I guess I do," Carol said, reluctant to leave. "Help me get out, Cat."

When they reached the door, Carol turned on Cat. "Cat, are you crazy? What are you doing? You can't let Mark stay here. Not just the two of you."

"Hush, Carol," Cat said, as she pushed her out the door. "I know what I'm doing. He didn't have anyone. He needed me and, frankly, I need him."

"You can't be serious, Cat," Carol said. "I thought you said you thought he killed Jim."

"I was mistaken," Cat said. "Now, go on home. I'll be fine."

"I don't like it, Cat," Carol persisted.

"It's OK, Carol," Cat said. "Just go on home."

She shut the door behind Carol and walked back into the kitchen.

"She doesn't like me much does she?" Mark asked.

"She'll get over it," Cat said. "It's my fault. You know I blamed you for Jim's death. I'm sorry that I did that, now, but I was crazy with guilt and grief. If I hadn't insisted on going on that assignment when Jim didn't want me to go, he would still be alive. It was all my fault that he died and I couldn't accept that fact. I had to have someone else to blame and you were the nearest one. I have to apologize to you, Mark. I know I made your life miserable. I hated myself and I couldn't stand it. It hurt too much to realize that I killed the one that I loved most in this world." Cat started to cry and Mark held out his hand in the direction he thought Cat was standing.

"It's OK, Cat," he said when he found her hand and squeezed it. "I was glad that I could help you vent your frustration. It hurt that you believed I had killed Jim when I had tried so hard to save him, but maybe I deserved the accuation. I'm not saying that I didn't do everything I could to save him, because I did. I'm just saying, maybe I should have insisted that he go first and let me cover you. That's all over now, though, and we can't go back and change it. No matter how much we wish we could, we still can't change it."

Cat was sobbing now. It was hard to stop crying. "Maybe we both have something to feel guilty for, Mark, but maybe time will heal us and we can get on with our lives," she said.

"Let's hope so," Mark said, then he was silent for a few minutes while Cat composed herself.

"Are you ready to go back to the den?" Cat asked.

"I am if you are," he answered.

"Here, let me help you get up," Cat said, as she put her arm around Mark's waist and steadied him so he could get up.

As they passed Jim's office, Mark sensed that they were near it. "Do you mind if I just go into Jim's office for a few minutes?" he asked.

"I haven't been in there since Jim's death.," Cat answered with tears in her eyes. "I didn't even look to see what it looked like after you took all of the FSC stuff out. I just couldn't make myself go in there. I hated that room. Jim spent too much time in there, time that I wasn't allowed to share. There were too many memories. It hurt too much. Yes, you can go in if you would like."

Cat opened the door and pointed Mark in the direction of Jim's desk. She stood in the doorway and watched as Mark found the desk and caressed the edges of it. He then made his way around to Jim's chair. He caressed the back of the chair then he cautiously sat down.

Cat stood and watched, as long as she could stand it and then walked back to the kitchen. After a while, she returned to the office to find Mark with his head on Jim's desk and he was sobbing just like she had done before. Cat stood and watched Mark for a few minutes without saying anything. She thought it was best to let him grieve. She knew how long it had taken her to come to grips with her loss and she realized now that Mark had lost Jim also. It was funny, she had never even thought that Mark had lost his best friend when Jim died. She knew that they were feuding just before Jim died, but she also knew that he still cared a great deal for Jim.

"Mark," she finally said softly. "Let's go back to the den." Then she went in and took his hand and led him back to the sofa.

Mark sat there for a long time not saying anything and Cat didn't want to intrude into his thoughts, so she just sat beside him and left him alone with his thoughts.

"Thanks, again, Cat," Mark finally said. "I appreciate what you're doing for me. I don't really have anyone who cares whether I live or die, not like Jim did. Everyone loved Jim, but my team really doesn't even respect me, I think. I would have had a hard time at the barracks. I think Ted's still mad because I made Commander and he thought he should have. The rest of the men go along with Ted. They think he should have been Commander, too. Now, he can be the Commander. I'll never be able to command my team ever again."

"You don't know that, Mark," Cat said. "The doctor said that sometimes it takes a couple of weeks for your eyes to adjust. This is only the first day."

"I know, Cat. I also know how I feel, and I feel that I'll never get well," he said.

"Mark, you never want to give up," Cat said, taking his hand and squeezing it. "I almost gave up, but someone cared for me and came and forced me to go to church. I didn't want to go, but if I hadn't, I would still be that same empty shell that I was three years ago. I appreciate what you did for me, Mark. You helped me to want to live again. I can never repay you for that. I'm going to do all I can to help you the same way. You'll see. It's not as bad as it seems. There is a light at the end of the tunnel."

"Cat, what I did for you, I did because I love you. You don't have to try to repay me. Just to know that what I did helped you is all the repayment I could ask for," Mark said.

Cat leaned over and gave Mark a quick kiss on the lips. He pulled her to him and kissed her back. Then he kissed her again, this time more urgently and passionately. He put all of his pent up love for Cat into his kiss. For a moment he forgot everything except his love for Cat.

"Wait, Mark," Cat said, as she shoved Mark back and stood up. "I didn't intend to start something that I couldn't stop. We have to take it a step at a time. First you have to court me. Then, after a while, when we know that we're really in love, you can ask me to marry you. I may say yes and then we'll get married. After that, we'll make love. We don't skip any steps."

"I'm sorry, Cat. I lost my head. Do you want me to leave?" Mark asked.

"No, Mark, of course not. I just want you to know how we stand. The courting comes first."

"Why would you want a blind, broken-down lover like me, anyway, Cat. I'm sorry that I overstepped my boundary. I'll try not to let it happen again."

"I think I better go on upstairs," Cat said. "Here, lie back and let me put these drops into your eyes."

After she put the drops into Mark's eyes, Cat went into the kitchen for a glass of water.

"Here, take this pill," she said. "It's your antibiotic. Do you need a pain pill?"

"It wouldn't hurt to take one," he answered. "I probably won't sleep without it."

"Here, take it," she said.

After he took the pill, she asked if there was anything else he needed.

"No, Cat. I'm sorry that I took advantage of your sympathy and forced myself on you," Mark said.

"You didn't do anything that I didn't want you to do, Mark. I'll see you in the morning. Good night."

Then she covered him up, turned out the light and ran upstairs to her bedroom.

Printed in the United States
By Bookmasters